J BOG WALKER

DEMCO

MADAM C.J. WALKER
Cookie Lommel

MELROSE SQUARE PUBLISHING COMPANY
LOS ANGELES, CALIFORNIA

COOKIE LOMMEL is a veteran news journalist, focusing on the entertainment industry. She started her writing career as a columnist for *Cash Box Magazine* and *Radio and Records*. She has also written for *Beverly Hills People, Palm Springs Life,* and *Teen Magazine.*

PICTURE CREDITS

Original drawing for Melrose Square by Christoper De Gasperi: p. 42; The Bettman Archive: p. 69; Florida State Archives: pp. 12–13, 15, 141; Indiana Historical Society: pp. 18–19, 76–77, 82, 95, 100, 106–107, 110–111, 116–117, 120, 128–129, 156–157, 164–165, 184–185; Library of Congress: pp. 8, 30–31, 46–47, 159, 160; Ray Locke: pp. 20, 40–41, 99; Maple Leaf Club: pp. 58–59; Missouri Historical Society: pp. 50–51; NAACP Public Relations: pp. 146–147; Neyland Collection: 26–27, 66; Players Magazine Archives; pp. 124–125, 142, 176; Private Collection: pp. 36–37; Duncan P. Schiedt: p. 137; The Schomburg Center for Research of Black Culture, New York Public Library, Astor, Lenox and Tilden Foundation: pp. 8, 30–31, 46–47, 159, 160; U.S. Department of Defense: p. 175.

Consulting Editors for Melrose Square
Raymond Friday Locke
James Neyland

Originally published by Melrose Square, Los Angeles.

All rights reserved under International and Pan-American Copyright Conventions. No part of this book may be reproduced in any form or by electronic or mechanical means including information storage and retrieval systems without permission in writing from the publisher, except by a reviewer who may quote brief passages in a review. Published in the United States by Melrose Square Publishing Company, an imprint of Holloway House Publishing Company, 8060 Melrose Avenue, Los Angeles, California 90046. ©1993 by Cookie Lommel.

Cover Painting: Jesse Santos
Cover Design: Bill Skurski

MADAM
C.J. WALKER

MELROSE SQUARE BLACK AMERICAN SERIES

ELLA FITZGERALD
singer
NAT TURNER
slave revolt leader
PAUL ROBESON
singer and actor
JACKIE ROBINSON
baseball great
LOUIS ARMSTRONG
musician
SCOTT JOPLIN
composer
MATTHEW HENSON
explorer
MALCOLM X
militant black leader
CHESTER HIMES
author
SOJOURNER TRUTH
antislavery activist
BILLIE HOLIDAY
singer
RICHARD WRIGHT
writer
ALTHEA GIBSON
tennis champion
JAMES BALDWIN
author
JESSE OWENS
olympics star
MARCUS GARVEY
black nationalist leader
SIDNEY POITIER
actor
WILMA RUDOLPH
track star
MUHAMMAD ALI
boxing champion
FREDERICK DOUGLASS
patriot & activist
MARTIN LUTHER KING, JR.
civil rights leader

CONTENTS

1
Women's Duty to Women 9

2
Childhood and Young Adulthood 23

3
From Laundress to Inventor 43

4
Starting the Business 67

5
Expansion and the Walker System 83

6
Peers 101

7
Dreams, Riches and War 121

8
Fulfilling a Need 143

9
Perseverance Was Her Motto 161

10
Unfinished Business 177

Chapter One

Women's Duty to Women

TWO HUNDRED WOMEN FROM all over the nation filled the room. Northern women, southern women, and women from the far western states gathered in Philadelphia for the first Madam C.J. Walker Hair Culturists Union of America convention. In 1917, the average Negro woman earned little more than a dollar a day—sometimes even only a dollar a week—as a maid or a laundress for a white employer. But by 1919, the 25,000 black women who worked as Madam Walker's agents could earn one thousand dollars daily, seven days a week. At one time, though,

Madam C.J. Walker as she looked in her early forties, shortly after she had begun to develop her hair and beauty products for African-American women.

Madam Walker's husband thought that she should be satisfied with earning ten dollars per day from her line of black hair care products.

But Madam C.J. Walker, born Sarah Breedlove, did not allow herself to be limited by narrow, stereotyped visions of what ought to satisfy a black woman in the racially segregated and sexist society of early twentieth century America. Instead, Walker addressed the Philadelphia convention on the subject of "Women's Duty to Women." "If women could develop a business, they could manage their lives," says her entry in *Notable Black American Women*. And if that business were to be as successful as that of Madam Walker, the first self-made female millionaire in the United States, a woman could substantially contribute to her family, her community, and her people.

But current prejudices about race and sex consigned women to the protection and support of men, and blacks to the exploitation and paternalism of whites. In 1863, the Emancipation Proclamation forbade slavery in the United States, but the Reconstruction era that followed the Civil War was a time of great misery and hardship for blacks. In the rural South, blacks officially became sharecroppers instead of slaves, but their actual living and working conditions improved little.

In addition to the problems facing most black Americans, Madam Walker also confronted—and overcame—prejudices limiting women's independence. Women did not even win the right to vote in the United States until the passage of the Nineteenth Amendment on August 18, 1920, but by 1914, the extraordinary Madam Walker had earned over a million dollars gross from her hair care business.

Madam Walker and other women did not find it good to rely on the traditional sex roles, which anticipated that they would be cared for by men. For one thing, most black women couldn't afford to. According to Stephen Gross in *Social Science History,* fifty-four percent of the black women who worked as domestic servants (cook, maid, laundress, etc.) were married. They combined exhausting fourteen-hour days with marriage and a family. Most had no choice. In the era following the Civil War, black women had a greater chance of finding employment as a domestic than freed black males had of working as hired labor.

But financial problems were not the only reason a woman wanted to earn her own living. After Madam Walker had begun her business, she married again. Her husband

In the South in the late nineteenth century, opportunities for blacks were limited. Most had traded slavery for another form of peonage, sharecropping. In this system, white landowners

took a percentage of what the sharecroppers grew in return for the "privilege" of barely subsisting and working on the property they were unable to own.

taught her marketing practices, but did not support her inner desire for greater opportunities. She told *New York Age,* "When I started in business...with my husband, I had business disagreements with him.... I was convinced that my hair preparations would fill a long-felt want, and when we found it impossible to agree, due to his narrowness of vision, I embarked in business for myself." Not satisfied with economic independence, Madam Walker had taught herself to read and write, and with the help of distinguished scholars such as Booker T. Washington, became knowledgeable in history and literature.

Madam Walker also stressed the importance of women's political participation. At the 1917 Madam C.J. Walker Hair Culturists' Union convention in Philadelphia, the Walker agents sent a telegram to United States President Woodrow Wilson to support a proposed federal anti-lynching law and to protest the recent murders of many blacks in East St. Louis, Illinois.

That telegram read, in part: "Honored Sir: ...Knowing that no people in all the world are more loyal and patriotic than the Colored people of America, we respectfully submit to you this our protest against the continuation of such wrongs and injustices and we further

Jobs for black women in the late nineteenth century were limited by stereotypes both of color and gender. Most were restricted to working as maids, cooks, and laundresses.

respectfully urge that you as President of these United States use your great influence that congress enact the necessary laws to prevent a recurrence of such disgraceful affairs."

President Wilson did not respond to the pleas of activists such as Madam Walker until a year later, and then he did not make a strong statement demonstrating resolution against prejudice. But Madam Walker showed courage in her pursuit of the necessary federal legislation, and set an example that her agents were proud to follow.

She won their affection and respect as few employers had previously done. Madam Walker's own experiences as a black woman in an unintegrated society were never forgotten as she pursued her dream of moving from the washtub to the boardroom. The doors that she opened up for herself were held open for other poor black women. Madam Walker knew how rare it was for blacks to be treated with the dignity all human beings deserve.

One of the reasons Madam Walker succeeded far better than other entrepreneurs in the black hair care market was that she addressed this need for respect. The Walker system of marketing her products, which would later be used by such modern companies as Tupperware and Mary Kay cosmetics, promoted something she called hair culture. Hair culture was a beauty ritual designed to make black women feel proud of their personal appearance. Madam Walker knew that it was easy for white employers to dismiss their raggedly groomed black employees as inferior, resulting in a low self-esteem shared by many blacks. But she also knew there were few ways of dressing black hair in the current long fashions. Women had to use dangerous hot irons or tightly wound papers and string to relax the hair, and it did scalp damage. Madam Walker herself invented her product, Wonderful Hair Grower, when her own hair began to fall out from stress and malnutrition, common problems for blacks.

Madam Walker also put her own photograph on her product. This marketing move was unusual; standards of beauty were Caucasian rather than Negroid, even in much of the black community, and it was rare to see a picture of anyone but a light-skinned black on a product's packaging. But Madam Walker knew that she could encourage black women to find a style and product for themselves.

Her whole approach to business incorporated the desire for respect. She called herself Madam C.J. Walker because her married title and the use of initials alone would

Some of Madam Walker's early products are displayed in the above photo, including soap, cleansing cream, vanishing cream, witch hazel jelly, cold cream, face powder, and perfume. All

were developed for the special needs of African-American women's hair and skin type, and some were aimed at curing problems from malnutrition and crude attempts to straighten hair.

prevent the traditional practice of whites calling all black women, no matter how unfamiliar or distinguished, by their first names.

Her agents were taught to create an atmosphere of respect and luxury in her beauty salons so that black women could go to them and have their own needs attended to. Madam Walker's "hair culture" aimed to make black women feel important and to feel beautiful inside as well as out.

In order to develop her business, she first peddled her products door to door, persevering through long sales trips. The approach was successful, and she eventually was able to commission a huge force of sales agents. Her sales force consisted of black women. Throughout her career, Madam Walker employed, and thus supported the dreams of, her people.

Her own dreams were realized in wealth and in the distinguished company that frequented her fantastic $250,000 mansion on the Hudson River in Irvington, New York. This cream-colored Georgian palace, the Villa Lewaro, was the site of many parties and dinners, and its furnishings were splendid. Her guests included many famous black artists, activists, professionals, and intellectuals, as well as many whites. Madam Walker saw this display, as she saw her business, as filling a need. Blacks needed to feel proud of what they could achieve, and her thirty-four room mansion was a symbol of what could be achieved with perseverance.

But Madam Walker did not spend her money solely on luxuries. She contributed to many black educational and charitable institutions, and has been remembered for her generosity. Throughout her sales career, she helped a number of her agents to raise the money to invest in her product, and employed black men in her manufacturing business.

Madam C.J. Walker's business and its famous Walker System continue to inspire black women everywhere. Her life was extraordinary and lived with a courage that defied prejudice and stereotypes. Yet it began with the same experiences that many black women of her time shared.

Chapter Two

Childhood and Young Adulthood

MADAM WALKER, BORN TO sharecroppers in 1867 Louisiana, worked from sunup to sundown picking cotton on the white Burney family plantation. Later, her life in the city of St. Louis, Missouri, was not much better. As a single mother, she struggled to support her daughter, Lelia, while working as a cook and a laundress. She spent long hours over the washtub, and then scrimped and saved money on necessities and on luxuries in order to have money for her daughter's education.

Because Madam Walker had to make her own fortune rather than inheriting wealth

Madam Walker was born Sarah Breedlove in 1867, near Delta, Louisiana, the daughter of sharecroppers who lived in a shack much like the one seen here.

from her family, she understood the experience of other black women of her time, both rural and urban. She understood their experiences because she had shared them as a child and as a young woman. During her early life as Sarah Breedlove, she was very familiar with hardship, poverty, and prejudice.

But she learned what she could from her difficult situation. The most important lesson was that women need to be able to rely on themselves to support a family and achieve their own dreams. Madam C.J. Walker was motivated by her experiences with bad times and worked hard to gain financial independence. She was also determined to share what she had learned so painfully. Madam Walker contributed much to her daughter's life and to improving the circumstances of the larger community of black women.

For her daughter's sake, she worked long hours. It was her desire that Lelia (who later changed to name to A'Lelia) should go to school, including college. Madam Walker did not have the opportunity to go to school herself until she was very much older. She prized the knowledge, comfort, and independence education can bring a young person.

Later, when her hair care product line began to show an astonishing profit, she also created financial opportunities for over 25,000 black women. These women were her sales force, the Walker agents so inspired by their founder. They believed in Sarah Breedlove McWilliams Walker because, at heart, she understood how important it was to improve their lives. For so many years, she had shared the grinding life of poverty and battled daily with prejudice. Sarah's early world was bleak and harsh.

Madam C.J. Walker was born Sarah Breedlove in a rundown shack in Louisiana on December 23, 1867. Her parents, Owen and Minerva Breedlove, had been slaves. When Sarah was born, they were working as sharecroppers on the plantation of Robert W. Burney, as they had done when they were still slaves. The Burney family lived in Delta, Louisiana, on the banks of the Mississippi River. Across the water, the city of Vicksburg could be seen from the Burney estate. Traffic on the river was constant, as transportation of goods such as cotton by riverboat was important to the economy of the South in 1867.

The life of a sharecropper was hard. The shack in which Sarah lived until she was seven had no windows, no running water, no electricity, and no indoor toilet. The heat in the summertime was nearly intolerable because the South is very hot and humid. Swamp-like

A view of Vicksburg, Mississippi, from across the river, near where Madam Walker spent her childhood. When she was seven years old, her parents died of yellow fever, and she and her

brother and sister moved to Vicksburg where they could find work. It was here that young Sarah began working as a washerwoman and married for the first time.

conditions bred mosquitos and other disease-carrying insects, and terrible illnesses were common. No child labor laws were enforced at that time, and small children worked from sunup to sundown alongside their parents, except for short seasons before planting and after harvesting when the children had some rough schooling. As a child, Sarah probably carried water for planting, dropped seeds in the rows made with plows by the older sharecroppers, helped cook for the family, dug potatoes, fed the chickens, and swept the laundry. On Saturdays, she and her mother and her older sister, Louvenia, got up at dawn to do the family laundry and to wash clothes for white people for about one dollar a week.

There was no money for extras. Every penny was needed to keep the family alive. Even the eggs from the chickens were sold for whatever income they would bring. As a child, Sarah received the material for one dress per year from the Burney family. Being patronized in such a way may have stung almost as much as the poverty.

Owen and Minerva Breedlove did not necessarily work as sharecroppers by choice. Life in the 1860s was very difficult for blacks, who were only beginning the very long road to genuine freedom. Blacks in the deep South of the United States, known as the Cotton Belt, faced the worst problems of all.

After the Civil War ended, a period known as Reconstruction began. Reconstruction, or the rebuilding of southern society and the southern economy after the devastation of the Civil War, took place during the period of 1865 to 1877. The 1880s were a time of change, and also a time of great peril, for blacks.

The changes legally began with the passage of the Thirteenth Amendment to the Constitution, which abolished, or ended, slavery. The Thirteenth Amendment reads: "Neither slavery nor involuntary servitude, except as punishment for crime whereof the party shall have been duly convicted, shall exist within the United States, or any place subject to their jurisdiction." This amendment meant that only criminals would be held against their will to work for someone else. The Thirteenth Amendment was passed on December 6, 1865.

But the Thirteenth Amendment was not nearly enough. It was one thing to say a person was no longer a slave and another thing for a black person to have the same rights as a white person. The Fourteenth Amendment, therefore, followed the Thirteenth. The Fourteenth Amendment, passed by Congress into law on July 9, 1868, declared that all persons

The Reconstruction era was a time of turmoil for African Americans. Some conditions improved for some freed slaves, but not for all, especially in Louisiana. Freedmen ran for

political offices, and a few were elected, but after federal troops left, the old-line whites regained power and placed restrictions on the rights and opportunities for blacks.

born in the United States, including former slaves, were citizens entitled to equal protection from laws unfairly restricting their freedom and limiting property ownership. Congress, the federal governing body, has supreme power over the laws of the land, including the laws individual states can make. This fact was especially important because many of the southern states tried to make laws that would take equal rights away from the Negro.

But the Thirteenth and Fourteenth Amendments still did not guarantee blacks a voice in their own government. In nineteenth century America, many groups did not have the vote. Women, for example, did not gain the right to vote until 1920. Black men gained it earlier, on paper, although in fact it was many years before blacks were fully guaranteed the right to express their opinions by voting.

The Fifteenth Amendment was ratified, or passed, by Congress on February 3, 1870. The Fifteenth Amendment said simply, "The right of citizens of the United States to vote shall not be denied or abridged by the United States or by any state on account of race, color, or previous condition of servitude. The Congress shall have power to enforce this article by appropriate legislation."

In this political cartoon, former Confederate President Jefferson Davis is depicted as horrified to see his former seat in the United States Senate occupied by a black man.

Unfortunately, congressional enforcement of the three amendments designed to make blacks and whites equal was not good enough to make a difference in the lives of southern blacks like Owen and Minerva Breedlove.

For example, despite the presence of two thousand soldiers in the state of Mississippi in 1869, an estimated twenty thousand black voters were discouraged from voting by racist groups such as the Ku Klux Klan, The White League, The Knights of the White Camellia, and the White Brotherhood. These terrible groups were responsible for the murders of over one thousand blacks in Louisiana between April and November of 1868. As a result, of the 26,814 black voters registered in April of that year, only 501 turned out to vote in the November elections. The presence of soldiers did not mean voters were safe. In 1873, the Colfax Massacre took place in Louisiana. The state militia, mostly black, came to battle with the racist-terrorist paramilitary group known as The White League. Seventy militiamen were killed. Over half of them were murdered in cold blood after surrendering.

Because federal laws promoting equality were not enforced, unfair state laws restricting the freedom of blacks like Owen and Minerva and young Sarah multiplied. In Louisiana, plantation owners often blocked freed blacks from owning property. Then, in 1867, black farmers were ordered to accept any work offered to them or they would be arrested and charged with vagrancy. This meant that Owen and Minerva continued to work on the plantation where they had once been slaves. They had little genuine choice.

The Reconstruction period was mostly dominated by financial concerns. The South relied upon slave labor to produce its cotton at a profit, and after the Civil War, it tried to continue doing the same. Blacks were paid so poorly to work the fields that they frequently could not escape falling into debt themselves. This, in turn, affected their chance to vote in a better system. Many southern states began levying something called poll taxes in order to discourage blacks from voting. Voters were required to pay poll tax in the spring, before they could see any profit from their harvests, if they wished to vote. The taxes were cumulative, so that each year they would have to pay for the previous year's debt as well as the new one before they could vote.

Blacks like the Breedloves did not have the money. The Civil War had made the South poor, and blacks the poorest of all. It took fifty years for the South to reach the income level

The Ku Klux Klan intimidated blacks in the South and in some cases killed them to try to keep them from participating in the political system. Sarah's first husband, Moses McWilliams,

father of her daughter Lelia, was killed in racial violence when Sarah was twenty years old, leaving her to struggle for survival on her own.

it had in pre-war years. In 1880, for example, the average southerner earned only two-fifths as much as the average northerner. The average black southerner earned half of that paid to southern whites. The North was investing less money in the South, and a decline in agriculture and manufacturing, coupled with a drop in the price of cotton, shattered the southern economy.

Madam Walker learned one very important lesson from the South of her childhood. To be free, you needed to be financially independent. You must be able to earn your own living or you would be condemned to a life that was slavery in all but name.

The miserable poverty in which they lived on the plantation affected Owen and Minerva's resistance to disease. They had poor nutrition and no medical care, so when a yellow fever epidemic swept Delta in 1874, Owen and Minerva both died of the illness. Sarah was only seven years old.

Her older brother, Alex, and her sister, Louvenia, tried to work the small farm, but could not. Alex decided to move across the river to Vicksburg to find work. Sarah and Louvenia were soon forced to move there, too. In 1878, yellow fever returned and three thousand people died. The cotton crops failed. The

Breedloves lost their home to debt.

In Vicksburg, Sarah and Louvenia took what work they could get as washerwomen and servants. Louvenia married a cruel man named Willie Powell who made Sarah's life a misery. She married at fourteen, probably to escape Powell. Sarah's first husband was Moses (Jeff) McWilliams, a Vicksburg laborer. Sarah and Moses had a daughter, Lelia, on June 6, 1885. Sarah was only seventeen. But when she was twenty, Sarah was a widow.

The cause of McWilliams' death is not certain. Some say he was killed in an accident. Others report that he was killed in a race riot or lynched at the hands of a white mob in Greenwood, Mississippi. During the terrible time between 1885 and 1916, over three thousand blacks were murdered by racist mobs. Later, Madam Walker would lobby strenuously for stronger anti-lynching laws.

Sarah lost first her parents, then the protection of her older brother Alex. She could not trust Willie Powell. Her own husband was tragically killed. She learned firsthand that the protection to be gained from living with males was not a stable thing. It could not be taken for granted. She must rely on herself to provide for her two-year-old daughter, Lelia. It was a lesson she tried to teach other women.

The town of Greenwood, Mississippi, as it is today. It was here that Moses McWilliams, Sarah's husband, was killed. One story is that he was lynched by whites, and that was the reason she

later began an anti-lynching crusade. It was certainly one of the reasons she decided to leave the South, first moving to St. Louis, then to Denver.

Chapter Three

From Laundress to Inventor

FINANCIAL SECURITY IS NOT the only reason a woman wants to be capable of earning her own living. Women, like men, need to feel a sense of self-worth. They need to fulfill their inner visions. But traditionally, women were not expected to follow their dreams, no matter how deeply they wanted to. In this respect, Madam C.J. Walker was different from many women of her era. She pursued her dream even when she received little encouragement, and later helped others to achieve theirs. But it was never easy.

In 1888, Sarah Breedlove McWilliams began

After the death of her husband, young Sarah was left to support her infant daughter on her own. She was determined that Lelia would have the opportunity to acquire an education.

working as a laundress in St. Louis, Missouri, after leaving Vicksburg. When her first husband died, Sarah was left in a difficult situation. She did not want to take her two-year-old baby, Lelia, to live with Louvenia and Willie Powell. It was getting harder and harder to find work in the rural South, whose economy was collapsing. Finally, her neighbors suggested that she try to find work in St. Louis, Missouri, which was a large urban area. They told Sarah that she had relatives there and that there were more jobs available. There were also higher wages, which was important to a single mother supporting a small child.

Sarah worked until she could buy a ticket north on the riverboat to St. Louis. She took Lelia to a rooming house in the black section of St. Louis, which was more prosperous than the black communities of the rural deep South. In St. Louis, over 35,000 of the city's half-million people were black. There were three black newspapers, and over one hundred black-owned businesses, a refreshing change from plantation life. The streets of St. Louis were "modern" too—they were lighted with electricity and gas.

But St. Louis was still not a paradise, especially for a black single mother. Wages were higher than in the South, but a black woman or man still did not earn nearly what a white worker earned. Sarah still had to work fourteen hours a day, doing white people's laundry and then walking to deliver it. Because she had a baby who needed her at home, Sarah could not find work as a domestic servant who lived in a white household. Instead, she worked as a laundress. She spent many hours every day bent over steaming washtubs, scrubbing mountains of soiled clothes, and then starching, ironing, and delivering them.

She eventually married her second husband. His name was John Davis, and little is known of him except that he was probably an alcoholic. They were divorced before Lelia finished high school.

Meanwhile, Sarah dreamed of a much better life. At first, it did not seem possible, even though Sarah began to further her own education. She attended public night schools in St. Louis and began saving money to send Lelia to college. It was hard to do because she had to deny herself not only luxuries but she had to skimp on the necessities sometimes, too. Sarah felt that her sacrifices were worthwhile, and throughout her life valued and promoted education for black women.

It was a very courageous position to take.

Sarah Breedlove made the move north to St. Louis by taking a steamboat up the Mississippi from Vicksburg. There she hoped

to start anew and to find opportunities to rise above working as a menial laborer despite her lack of education.

For one thing, the majority of the white community did not genuinely encourage the education of blacks. Most white schools did not admit black students. And in order to force blacks to remain illiterate and unable to vote in states with "literacy" clauses, racist groups such as the Ku Klux Klan burned black schoolhouses and killed or threatened those willing to teach black students. Before the Civil War, it had been illegal to teach a slave to read and write, and many bigoted people wanted to keep blacks from exercising any economic power. It is harder to keep a person powerless if that person is literate and understands their rightful place in the community.

Sarah's decision to send Lelia to Knoxville College, a small black school in Knoxville, Tennessee, was also unusual because she lived in an era where women were not expected to be well educated. Women, like blacks, were second-class citizens in nineteenth and early twentieth century America. Victorian conventions regarding women were linked to their biology, as arguments about the inferiority of blacks had been linked to the color of their skin. Because women's brains were smaller in size, they were therefore considered inferior to those of men, a belief which modern science does not support. The size of a brain has little to do with how accurately it functions, just as a small watch keeps the same time as a bigger watch.

Some scientists during the early twentieth century even warned that education would damage women and their unborn children. Even college presidents shared this ridiculous view. G. Stanley Hall, President of Clark University, said in his long-winded Victorian way in 1906, "Over-activity of the brain during the critical period of the middle and late teens will interfere with the full development of mammary power and of the functions essential for the full transmission of life generally."

Actually, the "critical period of middle to late teens" is a wonderful time to send a young woman to college, when she is just beginning to get excited about independence and about seeing more of the world. Men like Hall feared that women would not make the choices that men wanted them to make if women had a chance to fulfill their own dreams. Antifeminists argued that women had a natural place in the home, and a God-given obligation to fill that natural place.

But these anti-feminists, or chauvinists, who were even more common when Madam Walker was alive than they are now, failed to talk much

Upon arriving in St. Louis, Sarah set herself up as a laundress, but when the opportunity arose to work for African-American entrepeneur Annie Turnbo Malone, who was developing a line

of beauty products, she took it. Yet she had her own ideas about the beauty needs of blacks and made plans for developing a business based on her concepts.

about the fate of a black woman in society. Black women were told to stay at home, but they couldn't afford to. Even if they were married, they often had to be the major wage-earners in their families because black female domestic servants could earn more money than black males could earn as hired labor.

Single black mothers like Madam Walker had no choice at all. They could not remain at home tending to their households. They needed to be paid for their hard work. And in order to be lifted from their lives of poverty, black women needed a chance to be educated.

Madam Walker spent a lifetime creating such opportunities. Even at this point in her life, when she worked as a laundress, Madam Walker contributed to more than her daughter Lelia's life, although she was poor herself.

Her benevolent character revealed itself when she joined the St. Paul African Methodist Episcopal Church in St. Louis. St. Paul's had long been a rock of the black community. Prior to the Civil War, the church held a secret school that taught slaves to read and write, although it was illegal and the penalties for those who were caught were severe. St. Paul's also helped people in need, including Sarah Breedlove McWilliams when she first came to St. Louis. She helped others, in turn, as a member of St. Paul's Mite Missionary Society.

Her first charitable activities were later recorded by a local newspaper: "She read in the *Post Dispatch*...of an aged colored man with a blind sister and an invalid wife depending on him for support. Without acquaintance of any kind with the family, she went among friends in the behalf of the distressed people, succeeding in collecting $3.60 which she gave to them.... She felt it was her duty to do even more [so] she arranged for a pound party through which means groceries in abundance were given, also a purse of $7.50."

Through the Mite Missionary Society, she also met prominent black women for the first time. They made an important impression on her.

The 1904 World's Fair was held in St. Louis, Missouri, and it featured many speakers of importance to the black community. Booker T. Washington, a distinguished Negro educator, was there, as was his wife. Margaret Murray Washington, was an inspiration to Sarah Breedlove McWilliams. Margaret Murray Washington's appearance was dignified, and it struck Sarah that Mrs. Washington's grooming helped her to make a good impression. Her hair was neat and her clothes were clean and

Sarah admired Margaret Murray Washington, seen here in the front row seated next to her husband Booker T. Washington, for her dignity and her distinctively African-American style, and

Sarah patterned her standards of beauty on "Maggie" rather than on the currently popular white ideal, which was difficult even for most white women to meet.

well-pressed. She looked as though she were someone of importance.

Perhaps as early as the 1890s, Sarah had begun to think about the conditions necessary for a dignified appearance. Many black women did not have the tools available to make a good impression on their employers or on the world at large.

For one thing, blacks lived under conditions that made it difficult to maintain their appearance. Most had no running water, beauty supplies, or equipment.

One of the most common problems black women also had was hair loss. Malnutrition could cause hair to fall out in great quantities, and many poor black women suffered from this embarrassing and painful condition.

Black women also lost their hair for another reason. The dominant white culture valued straight hair, and most black women have hair that ranges from tightly curled to slightly wavy. In Africa, black hair was a source of pride. It was often highly ornamented and braided in many different patterns. But in America, shortly after the end of slavery, long straight hair was considered a sign of privilege and, therefore, a sign of respect and beauty. The black community was divided about how it ought to look.

Black preachers often wanted black women to wear their hair with its natural curls as a way to show pride in their heritage. They also thought that God wanted black women to look a certain way.

Other blacks, especially women, tried to straighten their hair. The usual way was painful and caused much hair loss. The hair would be sectioned off and then string would be wrapped tightly and twisted around each section. Upon combing, the hair would be straighter. It would also fall out.

Another method was to lay the hair on an ironing board or other flat surface and iron it straight. This method was dangerous as well as painful.

Madam Walker suffered from hair loss herself. She tried many available hair care products in order to stop the process of balding. Some of the hair care products, made from a variety of chemicals, caused more hair loss.

At some point, Sarah began to invent her own hair care products. She began with inventing a hair grower and thickener. Because of the debate over standards of black and white beauty, it was important to her that this product, the Wonderful Hair Grower, not be viewed as a straightener specifically because she

The World's Fair in St. Louis in 1904 focused attention not only on the city that was Sarah's new home but also on new products and scientific advances, making her aware of future

possibilities. It was at the fair that Sarah heard the inspirational words of Booker T. Washington and saw his wife Margaret for the first time.

wanted the respect of the black community. She said to a reporter, "Let me correct the erroneous impression held by some that I claim to straighten hair. I deplore such an impression because I have always held myself out as a hair culturist. I grow hair.... I want the great masses of my people to take a greater pride in their appearance and to give their hair proper attention."

Her own story of the invention of the Wonderful Hair Grower recalls a sense of African heritage. She told her friends that she asked God for help in stopping the hair loss, and that God answered her. "One night I had a dream, and in that dream a big black man appeared to me and told me what to mix up for my hair. Some of the remedy was grown in Africa, but I sent for it, mixed it, put it on my scalp, and in a few weeks, my hair was coming in faster than it had ever fallen out. I tried it on my friends; it helped them. I made up my mind I would begin to sell it."

Her secret ingredient was probably sulphur, a chemical that can heal some infections. In addition, she also invented or modified a special comb that would help straighten hair. This comb was made of steel and the teeth were spaced in order that blacks could use it more easily on their hair. When it was heated

This advertisement for Madam Walker's hair products appeared in The Messenger, *published by A. Philip Randolph, helping spread her market well beyond her initial neighborhood efforts.*

and a special softening ointment applied to it, hair could be manipulated with fewer problems. These combs were manufactured to her specifications in France where a prototype used by white women already existed. Madam Walker may have first seen hot combs in her childhood in Louisiana.

Once Madam Walker had created these products, historical sources disagree as to what she did next. According to at least one version, she began her hair care business in St. Louis, Missouri, where she sold her steel comb and her hair thickening formula, along with five or six other products that she developed sometime during this period, door to door.

Her first customers were herself, her friends, and perhaps the black community of St. Louis, although it was not completely certain where she first marketed her Wonderful Hair Grower.

Madam Walker, however, was not the only black woman who had an interest in black hair care. In the first months of 1905, she worked for Annie Turnbo Malone's company, Poro. "Poro" is a West African word. It means an "organization dedicated to disciplining and enhancing the body physically and spiritually." In 1902, Annie Turnbo Malone's hair care business had expanded to new quarters at 2223 Market Street in St. Louis. Madam Walker, still Sarah Breedlove McWilliams Davis then, began to work for Malone sometime prior to her invention of the Wonderful Hair Grower in 1905. Former Poro employees have said that Madam Walker may have had Malone's secret lotion, also called the Wonderful Hair Grower, analyzed. Madam Walker, though, later asserted that the hair treatments she had tried previous to inventing her own, including that of Malone's, didn't work.

Madam Walker's great-great-granddaughter, A'Lelia Perry Bundles, disputes Poro's claim to have originated the Wonderful Hair Grower sold by Madam Walker. A'Lelia says that Madam Walker even left St. Louis before pursuing her business, perhaps because she did not want to compete with her former employer. Madam Walker was divorced from John Davis by then, and had few ties to keep her in St. Louis.

According to A'Lelia Perry Bundles' account, Madam Walker may have had one important friend in St. Louis, however. She may have already met Charles Joseph Walker, the man who would later become her husband and an early driving force behind her successful marketing strategy. Charles Joseph Walker was a sales agent for a local black newspaper, and he had important ideas for mail-order marketing and advertising.

Although it is difficult to determine absolutely where Madam Walker got her ideas for her Wonderful Hair Grower and the steel comb, whether her business began in Denver or in the black neighborhoods of St. Louis, or indeed if she knew C.J. Walker first in Missouri or in Colorado, her contributions are nevertheless noteworthy. Joan Curl Elliott, writing for *Notable Black American Women,* puts the situation into a helpful perspective:

> Like most inventors, no one is totally original, for the inventor responds to a situation, improves upon it, and draws from the environment around him or her. Walker was not the first to organize a hair preparations company, since Annie Turnbo Malone with her Poro Company and "Wonderful Hair Grower" preceded her in 1900. Some sources suggest that Walker was first an agent for Malone and later her rival in the beauty empire business. Walker was also not the first to heat a comb to straighten hair since the French Jews pressed hair in the early eighteenth century. Nor was she the first to send products through the mail, for many white companies had used this strategy with much success. In fact, her husband, Charles Walker, recommended the idea from his experiences with

the newspaper business and advertisements. However, she was the first woman to organize supplies for black hair preparations, develop a steel comb with teeth spaced to comb the strands of blacks, place the comb on a hot stove, send the products through the mail, organize door-to-door agents, and develop her own beauty school. From a combination of these ideas, she nursed her company and it grew.

―――― *Chapter Four* ――――

Starting the Business

IN 1905, SARAH BREEDLOVE Mc-Williams moved to Denver, Colorado, an important step for her future as an entrepreneur. The most obvious reason for her move was the death of her older brother, Alex. He left behind a grieving widow and four daughters. Alex's family lived in Denver, and after Alex died, Sarah joined them. She was thirty-seven when she left the South for the first time.

It has also been suggested that she moved to Denver in order to avoid pitting her fledgling business against those such as Annie Turnbo Malone's Poro Company. The reasons

---

White standards of beauty were difficult for African-American women to follow, especially in regard to hair styles. Early techniques for straightening hair could lead to serious damage.

for her move could be numerous, but the result was simple: Unparalleled opportunity awaited her, and she was quick to take advantage of it.

Unlike the South, which suffered from a lack of manufacturing facilities and cash investment, Denver was sharing in the industrial boom known as the Gilded Age. Life in the urban North and West was far better than it was in the rural South at this point. The reason was the development of the railroad.

Between 1865 and 1880, railroad construction expanded across the United States from the Pacific Ocean to the Atlantic Ocean. Coal fueled the railroads and the industrial North and West could supply the coal. They could also mass produce steel to make railroad tracks.

Refrigeration was also a new invention. Hand in hand with the railroad, it changed the economy of the North and West because refrigerated railroad cars made it possible to carry fruits, vegetables, and meat for long distances. This benefited ranches, and huge cattle empires grew and spread across the West. Meat packing industries blossomed and prospered.

This Gilded Age was a time of unusual opportunity and prosperity. Wonderful new inventions included the typewriter, the tele-

With the spread of the railroad throughout the United States, the merchandising of everything from beef and farm produce to medication and beauty supplies became easier.

phone, electric light, and the phonograph. Travel, thanks to the railroads, was easier and cheaper. Shrewd business people who could fill a consumer need could develop monopolies. And more and more people were asking for luxury items which had previously been out of their reach.

Sarah Breedlove McWilliams came to Denver on July 21, 1905. She came by train, arriving at the Union Depot. She marveled at the change from St. Louis, her granddaughter says. Denver was mountainous with clear skies and none of the humidity of the South, which Sarah had known since birth.

There were less than ten thousand blacks in the city of Denver, but Colorado as a whole did not have much population. Importantly, Colorado had never been a slave state, and although discrimination certainly existed everywhere at this time, it was not as hard for Sarah to begin a business here as it would have been in her native Louisiana.

But it would be two years before Sarah could live from the proceeds of that business, the hair care empire. At first, she took a job as a cook. She may have worked for E.L. Scholtz, a pharmacist from Canada. He owned a large well-known drug store which sold both prescription medicine and home remedies.

It was a shrewd move on Sarah's part. Mr. Scholtz may have been consulted about the ingredients in the products that Sarah was developing, or had developed in St. Louis.

At night, Sarah Breedlove McWilliams and her nieces experimented with formulas. Finally, Sarah used her savings of one dollar and fifty cents (or even one dollar and twenty-five cents, according to once source) to market her products.

Those products were the Wonderful Hair Grower, Glossine, Vegetable Shampoo, Temple Grower, and Tetter Salve. She also marketed the heatable steel comb with the specially spaced teeth.

Her hair articles combined pharmaceutical uses with grooming. The Temple Grower and Tetter Salve were supposed to help cure psoriasis of the scalp, an uncomfortable condition that could lead to patchiness. The Wonderful Hair Grower, of course, was designed to restore the hair lost by so many blacks because of diet and circumstance. Glossine was a hair oil that would keep hair manageable.

During this time, as early as six months after she came to Denver, Sarah Breedlove McWilliams married newspaperman C.J. Walker. The ceremony took place on January

4, 1906. Walker had advised Sarah Breedlove McWilliams by mail from St. Louis, according to A'Lelia Perry Bundles, and then he came to Denver. They decided to marry.

Sarah Breedlove McWilliams then became known for business purposes as Madam C.J. Walker. Her adoption of this name was important to her self-respect because black women were generally addressed by their first names by whites of all ages, even if those whites were complete strangers. It was difficult to maintain a sense of professional dignity in the face of such condescending behavior. Accordingly, black women often kept their first names a secret, or used initials, so that they could not be addressed so familiarly.

Madam Walker understood the need of blacks for the same dignity given to the majority of whites. She knew that her race needed models to improve their self-esteem, and business opportunities to improve their circumstances. She also knew that improving the personal appearance of a black man or woman would increase their chances of finding good employment. Her hair care business was designed to meet this need, and in this way was a tremendous service to her people.

Madam Walker began as she meant to go on. Her products were packaged with pictures of herself and later her daughter. Besides being good advertisements for the efficacy of the hair growing products, because by now she had a head of thick, healthy hair, the packaging also flew in the face of common practice. During this period, dark-skinned blacks were not used as models because standards of beauty were white. Light-skinned blacks who looked whiter than their darker counterparts were more commonly used to sell products. Madam Walker, not particularly light-skinned herself, used her own picture anyway. The black community responded with favor.

To pay for her beginning business and her rent and necessities, Madam Walker still worked as a laundress for two days a week. The other days, she mixed her products in the big laundry tubs and then sold them door to door.

She gave her customers free demonstrations. She would wash a customer's hair with Vegetable Shampoo and then apply Wonderful Hair Grower. She followed it with Glossine, the hair oil, and then used a heated comb to finish. The results were evidently very pleasing as women began to respond to her sales campaign.

Madam Walker gave some care to her own appearance as she firmly believed it was one of her best assets. She would wear a long skirt in a dark color and a freshly ironed and starched white blouse. Her hair, of course, was well cared for. She carried her products in a black case.

Madam Walker's first profits had to be reinvested in her business. The money went on more raw materials for mixing her formulas and on advertising her wares. She put advertisements in a preeminent black newspaper published in Denver, the *Colorado Statesman,* and those advertisements began to spawn mail orders. Along with her personal sales trips, her business was beginning to promise a profit.

Madam Walker's husband was familiar with mail order and newspaper sales and he helped her expand her product line to include C.J. Walker's Blood and Rheumatic Remedy, a non-hair care product that was supposed to restore health to sufferers from blood and rheumatic disorders. They also changed the name of Wonderful Hair Grower to Madam C.J. Walker's Wonderful Hair Grower.

But there were problems with the marriage. Madam Walker had relied on herself for many years. She finally saw a chance to fulfill herself by developing her hair care business. She was making a profit of ten dollars per week when her husband decided that the business had met its full potential. Madam Walker believed, instead, that she should begin to market her product all over the United States rather than just in Denver and proposed a sales trip to open new markets. Her husband did not want her to go. He did not think she would even be able to pay for her trip with its profits. Madam Walker decided to go on her sales trip. She had a dream to fulfill. She traveled for over a year and a half. She visited nine states. These included her home state of Louisiana, Mississippi, Oklahoma, and even New York, a big market.

Eventually, she began to make thirty-five dollars a week, an unheard of salary for a black woman. White men earned less than half of that. Black women earned twenty times less than that, usually.

But the tensions in her marriage were apparent. She later told the *New York Age,* "When I started in business...with my husband, I had business disagreements with him, for when I began to make ten dollars a day, he thought that amount was enough and that I should be satisfied. But I was convinced that my hair preparations would fill a long-felt want, and when we found it impossible to agree, due to his narrowness of vision, I em-

After moving her business to Pittsburgh, Pennsylvania, Madam Walker established Lelia College there in 1908 to teach the beauty techniques she had developed. She named the school for

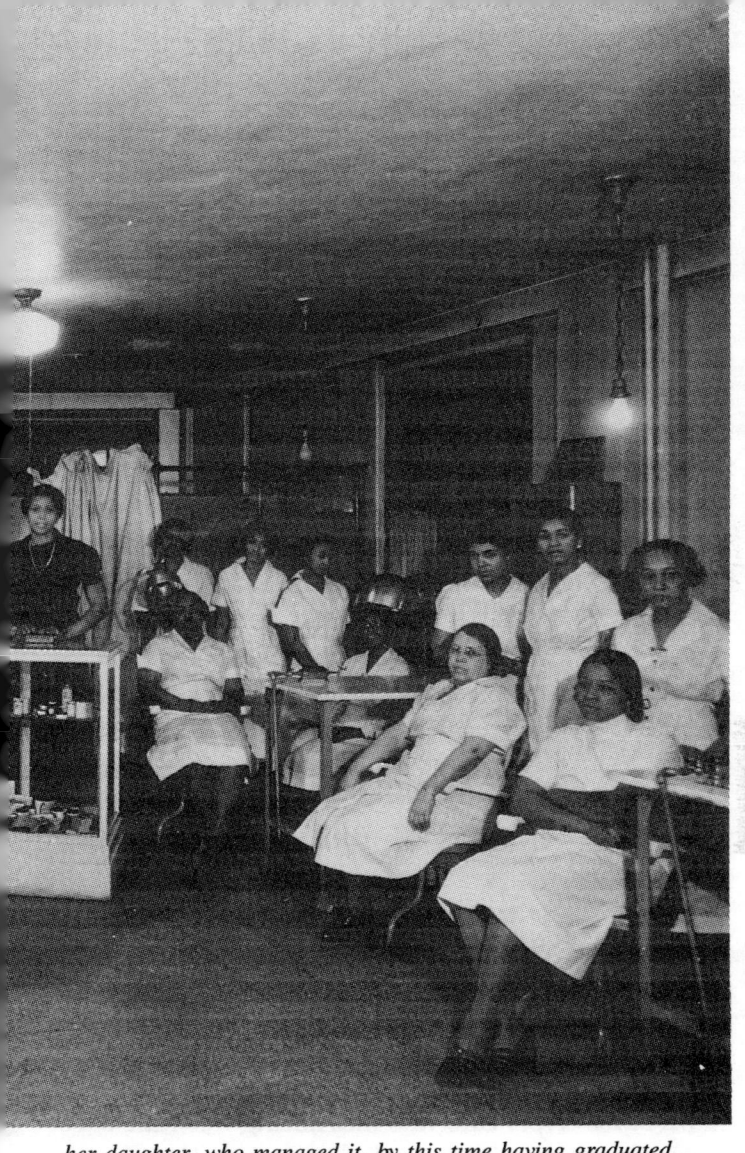

her daughter, who managed it, by this time having graduated from college. Eventually Lelia changed her name to A'Lelia, but the college name remained the same.

barked in business for myself."

It was not enough for Madam Walker to have her husband define her dreams. She wanted to spread her wings and find out for herself what potential existed in the marketplace. Sadly, the arguments persisted between Madam Walker and her third husband, and she filed for divorce in late 1912. She kept C.J. Walker's name.

In 1906, Madam Walker had a new helper for her business. Her daughter Lelia had just graduated from Knoxville College. Madam Walker put the twenty-one-year-old, whose education was very impressive considering that few blacks could read or write, in charge of her mail-order operation.

Lelia was an impressive addition to the company. She was nearly six feet tall and had a distinctive poise. Later, she would become a celebrated figure in the social circuits of the Harlem Renaissance. Lelia was very good at business, but even with the help of her cousins, Anjetta, Matti, Gladis, and Thirsapen, the mail orders were piling up.

Madam Walker herself was still hard at work on sales trips. She was marketing her hair care products as she traveled through the South and the East United States. She had also begun to teach her hair care methods, an important step for the expansion of the business.

Madam Walker began training agents to sell for her. In return for demonstrating and taking orders for hair care products, the agents received a commission, or share of the profits. In 1908, she signed up dozens of agents and her company began making a profit of four hundred dollars a month. This sum was vast by the standards of 1908.

Madam Walker decided to move her business to a more central location. After many sales trips, she selected Pittsburgh, Pennsylvania. Pittsburgh was closer to the greater population centers in the United States, which were still mostly northeastern.

Pittsburgh was a center of banking and manufacturing, especially steel. The steelworks were a boon in the making of the Walker heated comb. Pittsburgh had a growing black population, which Madam Walker saw as an opportunity to do something both for her business and for her people.

In Pittsburgh in 1908, she established a beauty parlor and a center for training agents, Lelia College. Graduates of her courses, almost all women, were called hair culturists. Her daughter also ran a correspondence course, or a course by mail, which cost twenty-five dollars. Scholarships and loans made it possible for poor black women to participate. Black women suddenly had an alternative to becoming cooks, laundresses, and house servants, and the potential to earn more money than even whites commonly earned. Supposedly, a hair culturist could make more in a week than a black would normally be able to make in a month. For this alone, she is remembered with tremendous gratitude.

But Madam Walker also encouraged her graduates to contribute to charity themselves. She gave prizes to the most benevolent, later as much as fifty dollars.

As one admiring observer put it so eloquently, "Keen of observation, she noted that millions of dollars were spent by our people annually for toilet requisites, that nearly all of these millions were going to the man who did not help colored charities or employ colored boys and girls. Madam Walker realized that in this as well as in other fields the Negro could make jobs for himself by establishing his own institutions and patronizing them and thus bring his dollars to his own pockets. Sensing this and realizing yet a bigger thing that if the Negro is to move forward as a desirable citizen he must have a care as to his personal appearance, she stepped out on the firing line and gave to her race the great company that bears her name and to-day stands out as foremost among the best."

Madam Walker's offices were on Wylie Avenue in Pittsburgh. Wylie Avenue was home to the more prosperous of the black community, including five lawyers, twenty-two doctors, and forty-five churches.

In 1910, Madam Walker was the subject of a feature article in the *Pennsylvania Negro Business Directory*. Madam Walker was called "one of the most successful businesswomen of the race in this community." She had accomplished a tremendous amount in the four short years, but the future of Madam Walker's business would be even more astonishing.

―――――― *Chapter Five* ――――――

Expansion and the Walker System

LELIA COLLEGE IN PITTSBURGH, Pennsylvania, was a great success. Graduates of the correspondence course at Lelia College received diplomas signed by Madam C.J. Walker, President, and Lelia Walker Robinson, Secretary. Robinson was Lelia's married name.

But, more importantly, graduates of the beauty college also received sales contracts. These contracts enabled these graduates to set up beauty shops of their own or work as agents for the Walker business. Madam Walker supplied the necessary metal tools and ointments to her graduates. The agents received aston-

By the time of her marriage, A'Lelia Walker Robinson had grown into a very striking beauty. Almost six feet tall, she dressed distinctively, even flamboyantly at times.

ishing profits in commissions from their sales of the Madam C.J. Walker Hair Grower, hot comb, Vegetable Shampoo, Glossine, and other hair care products. According to some former agents, these mostly black women could earn up to seven thousand dollars a week selling door to door.

The door-to-door method of sales had been used already by another beauty products company, Avon (which still markets in this fashion). Other companies would later employ this strategy for reaching women, the primary consumers of beauty products. Mary Kay Ash, for example, successfully used this method to build her modern cosmetics empire.

But commissioning agents was not the only tactic Madam C.J. Walker used to increase the volume of her business. She took advantage of her uncommon business sense and developed several other profitable ideas.

First, she wanted to be able to reach her potential customers. Although Pittsburgh had been a good location for Lelia College, Madam Walker envisioned an even more successful location for her company's headquarters. She was traveling constantly in order to market her product, while Lelia managed the beauty school, the manufacturing of the products, and the mail-order market which her sales trips

Because of her own lack of an education, Madam Walker had great admiration for African Americans like Mary McLeod Bethune who had dedicated their lives to educating others of their race.

and advertising developed. During one of her sales trips, she decided that Indianapolis, Indiana, was a convenient, centrally located city in the United States. Indianapolis also had readily available transportation facilities. From Indianapolis, she could conduct her promotional work for her hair care business more easily. It would be possible to reach more women from Indianapolis, a crucial point if she was to develop her business on a national level.

In 1910, Madam Walker moved her company's headquarters to Indianapolis. She also invested her growing profits in order to make some of her other business ideas a reality.

In order to ensure a steady supply of hair care products and to keep costs and other important parts of her business under her own control, Madam Walker built her own factories and laboratories. She furnished these facilities with the most up-to-date equipment available.

These manufacturing plants provided jobs for many Negro men. Madam Walker, sensitive to the needs of her people, paid good wages. In addition, she provided decent housing for her workers, a rarity in the Industrial Age. At this time in history, the majority of factory workers, white or black, were exploited by their employers. Labor laws were rare and difficult to enforce. An employer like

Madam Walker agreed with the philosophy of education espoused by Booker T. Washington, believing it was important for black men and women to learn trades and skills to advance economically.

Madam C.J. Walker was all the more special because she created a caring environment in a time when few people would have expected one.

In addition to building factories, filling mail orders, and certifying commissioned agents, Madam C.J. Walker dreamed of making a place where black women could go, even if just for a little while, and forget the harsh circumstances that most of them normally faced. Her beauty parlors were designed to make black women feel pampered and beautiful. She did this in order to help black women feel the sense of dignity and self-worth that can come when you feel that your needs are important. She trained her cosmeticians to provide an atmosphere of luxury and respect for Walker customers.

The beauty parlors, not surprisingly, were a great success. As she had with the invention and marketing of her hair care products, Madam Walker filled a need. Her own early years of poverty allowed her to instinctively understand that need, and she used her intuition to catapult her business into a phenomenal success. Between 1910 and 1919, Madam Walker set up a chain of beauty parlors throughout the United States.

She also expanded her business to an international level. Sales trips to the Caribbean and South America, which had large populations of blacks, convinced her that her beauty products would be well received in those areas, too. She set up beauty parlors throughout the West Indies and South America, and commissioned even more agents.

Madam Walker also began selling her goods in drug stores. Her business methods had diversified tremendously, and now included door-to-door sales, mail-order sales, drug store sales, beauty salons, and manufacturing facilities.

In fact, by 1910, Madam C.J. Walker's hair care business commissioned an estimated five thousand agents. By 1919, some figures report that there were 25,000 Walker agents. Her business had become an empire.

The empire was wildly successful, financially. Initially, Madam Walker had reinvested her profits, building her company from the ground up, so that all aspects of production and sales were under her watchful eye. But eventually, Madam Walker had profits left over—astonishing profits for a black woman in an era when women had few property rights and could not even vote.

Although some argue the fact, most consider Madam C.J. Walker to have been the first self-made female millionaire, black or white, in the United States.

The figures available are impressive, if they are to be believed. In September 1911, Madam C.J. Walker incorporated her company, making herself the sole stockholder. Between 1911 and 1917, she was probably making $100,000 per year. In 1917, sales of equipment and supplies had amounted to nearly $200,000 per year in profit. Her yearly payroll may have reached over two hundred thousand dollars per year.

But Madam C.J. Walker was creating more than profits. She was also creating opportunities and public services.

Many of her former employees have recalled Madam Walker with a sense of gratitude and even awe. She changed the lives of the people around her with both her amazing energy and her seemingly limitless compassion.

Peg Fisher, for example, was a secretary to Madam Walker's company attorney and general manager, Freeman B. Ransom. Peg Fisher told Jill Nelson, Freeman B. Ransom's granddaughter, that Madam Walker was "beautiful, just beautiful. I don't mean just physically beautiful; I mean beautiful in her ways. She had her shortcomings, but she surrounded herself with people of education who could be teaching her every minute; she was quick to catch on. And she was lovely to know." (*Essence,* June 1983.)

Other Walker employees and associates speak of Madam Walker with the same warmth. Lucille Wilson, who began working for the Walker cosmetics empire after Madam Walker had died in 1919, remembers the affection of those who had known the great woman. Ms. Wilson recalls, "All of the Madam C.J. Walker agents had a great love for Madam."

Lucille Wilson explains part of the affection as gratitude. Madam Walker changed their lives in the most basic way possible, by showing her employees a way out of hated poverty. Ms. Wilson says, "They felt she had given them an opportunity to make a living for themselves, which was different from the living that most colored women were able to make at that time." (*Essence,* June 1983.)

Former Walker agent Marjorie Joyner remembers how appealing it was to work for Madam Walker. In an era where many black women had parents who could remember slavery, Madam Walker's schools promised a freedom of movement that was glittering in comparison. Amazingly, Madam Walker could offer these opportunities because she had perceived the needs of many of her people and found a way to fill them.

"People would want to become agents and learn the trade so they could travel. They found out that they could make money plus have a new way of getting away from home," Marjorie Joyner says.

And what exotic travel! Few ordinary people in the early twentieth century, black or white, had the chance to visit foreign countries, and for formerly poverty-stricken black women, working for Madam Walker must have seemed like a dream. It certainly left an unerasable impression on her former agents.

"I traveled for Madam Walker to all the West Indian Islands, plus Paris, London, Rome, West Africa, and the Holy Land. There was an open market in those countries because no one there, at that time, was dressing colored people's hair," Ms. Joyner reminisced to Jill Nelson.

Part of Madam Walker's perceptiveness came from her naturally alert and questioning mind. Throughout her life, and later her dazzling career, Madam Walker had an unequaled zest for knowledge. She never passed up an opportunity to better herself. She admired education and was smart enough to know that a person never gets too old to learn new things. Madam Walker didn't just create opportunities for other people. She made the most of her own success.

Violet D. Reynolds revealed much about Madam Walker's never-ending thirst for knowledge. Ms. Reynolds began working as Walker's secretary in 1914 and worked her way up to Chairman of the Board before she retired in 1981, another impressive story. Ms. Reynolds remembered Madam Walker's drive to educate herself: "She'd come down every morning to read the paper in the office, and when she'd run into a word she didn't know what it meant or how to pronounce it, we would have to look it up and tell her." (*Essence,* June 1983.)

It was probably no accident that Madam Walker surrounded herself with people who were educated and could guide her own self-expansion. She understood the importance of surrounding herself with people who were interested in furthering her knowledge and welfare, and selected her acquaintances with care.

For example, Ms. Reynolds explained the mutual benefit to be gained from Madam Walker's friendship with Mary McLeod Bethune, a respected scholar and educator as well as an early black political activist. Ms.

Reynolds told Jill Nelson that Madam Walker "really respected education because she lacked it. That's why she was so attracted to Mary McLeod Bethune. Mrs. Bethune had the education, but Madam had the money, so they made a good team."

Booker T. Washington, also a respected black scholar and political spokesman, was another friend to Madam Walker. Washington tutored Madam Walker privately after she moved her company headquarters to Indianapolis.

Altogether, Madam Walker had come a long way from the washtubs of Missouri and Mississippi. Once she had been poor and illiterate, but by 1911, she was wealthy and well on her way to possessing an impressive education. She read widely and voraciously on her own, familiarizing herself with classical literature, history, and the academic achievements of the day. She understood the business world inside and out, and was educating herself politically so that she could shift the battleground for equal rights from economics to the law.

The expertise that she did not possess herself was sought in others. One of her most famous and valued employees was Freeman Briley Ransom.

About 1910, Madam Walker met Freeman B. Ransom, a law student. After he finished his education, she brought him to work for her company in Indianapolis, where he became her right-hand man.

During her travels in 1910 or 1911, she met a train porter. He impressed her immediately. The train porter was a law student at Columbia University in New York, and he was working hard during his school vacations in order to finance his education. Madam Walker recognized a kindred spirit. That train porter was Freeman B. Ransom.

Ransom was born in Grenada, Mississippi, on July 13, 1882. Before attending Columbia University, he studied theology at Walden University in Nashville, Tennessee.

Ransom was well educated and understood the law. He was not afraid to help Madam Walker in the dangerous fight for equality. He understood organization. In 1911, Madam Walker hired Freeman B. Ransom after he completed his education. He had taken a room in her house in Indianapolis. Ransom became the company attorney and general manager of the Walker company in Indianapolis. The arrangement suited Madam Walker greatly. She was free to travel as she liked, making contacts with the thousands of women who would become her agents and supporters. Ransom gave her invaluable help in incorporating her company, and in gaining a divorce for Lelia from her first husband, John Robinson.

Because Ransom could manage the Indianapolis headquarters, Madam Walker's daughter Lelia was able to move to New York in 1913. New York was a huge city by early twentieth century standards, and it represented an important market to the hair care and cosmetics empire. Influential people lived in New York, and as Violet Reynolds remembers, Madam Walker "had a knack for meeting influential people." So did her daughter, Lelia, who opened a second Lelia College and beauty salon in New York. Lelia opened the college and salon in her Harlem townhouse, which would later become the site of many expensive and glittering parties.

Lelia also took her adopted daughter, fourteen-year-old Mae, to New York. Continuing the family tradition, Mae worked in the New York operation as well as modeling for Madam Walker sometimes when Madam Walker traveled.

Madam Walker put her own personal stamp on all of her business. Agents were instructed to teach their customers about the value of good grooming and of personal hygiene. It would help black women overcome negative stereotypes and enable them to feel better about themselves.

In 1916, Madam Walker created the National Beauty Culturists and Benevolent

Association of Mme. C.J. Walker Agents. The name of this group was later changed, in 1917, to the Madam C.J. Walker Hair Culturists Union of America, but its purposes remained the same. Prizes were given for the highest levels of charitable and philanthropic work. The dependents of Madam Walker's agents were also not forgotten. Members of the union each paid twenty-five cents a month, so that when an agent died, her beneficiaries or family would receive fifty dollars to help make ends meet.

Madam Walker never forgot what it was like to be left on her own, poverty stricken, as a child. Her service clubs helped to ensure that fewer black children had to survive that nightmare. It is hardly remarkable that she is remembered with so much gratitude and affection.

Freeman Briley Ransom was born in Grenada, Mississippi, not far from where Madam Walker spent her youth. The similarity in their backgrounds helped enable them to work closely together.

―――――― *Chapter Six* ――――――

Peers

THE LIFE AND CAREER of Madam C.J. Walker was extraordinary. She accomplished more in her relatively short life than most people dream about. A great deal of credit is owed to her own energy and compassion. As a poor woman in the Reconstruction South and as a single mother, she faced tremendous personal odds and overcame them to be a success in the beauty business.

But it does not detract from her success to examine the other black women who also were successful in the hair care business in the early twentieth century. These women were Madam

---

A'Lelia's adopted daughter Mae, Madam Walker's only grandchild, was hired by the Walker Company as a model to appear in advertisements for the beauty products.

C.J. Walker's peers, and their lives help to explain Madam Walker's. No one lives in a historical or cultural vacuum. The careers of two other black women who achieved success in the beauty field demonstrate even more forcefully the window of opportunity that existed in the early twentieth century marketplace.

This window of opportunity clearly existed within the black marketplace. Black women were beginning to show that they could be important as a consumer force. Any business person who met their needs affordably might expect at least moderate success.

This consumer force was still new, however. It was created in the increasing prosperity that ushered in the urban age of late nineteenth century and early twentieth century America. Black women still did not earn much, compared to other segments of the population, but they were beginning to have small savings that could be spent on personal items rather than merely necessities. Between 1890 and the census in the 1920s, disposable personal income increased for all segments of the population.

This new consumer group of black women needed role models. These role models would define what women would spend their small extra incomes to get. Madam C.J. Walker was one of those role models. She firmly believed that it was worth the expenditure for a black woman to invest in her personal appearance. Two other pioneers of the beauty world shared her belief, and together with Madam C.J. Walker, they successfully convinced black women to buy their appearance-enhancing products.

The two pioneers who stand beside Madam C.J. Walker as her peers are Annie Turnbo Malone, founder of Poro Company, and Sarah Spencer Washington, founder of Apex Hair and News Company.

Annie Turnbo Malone is the more controversial figure for a biography of Madam C.J. Walker because she founded her beauty business before Madam Walker founded hers, and because there is some question as to who originated some of the products and methods both employed. It might be a more worthwhile perspective, however, to recognize that the scope of the black marketplace that was just opening up left room for both women to be wildly successful, both as businesswomen and as philanthropists.

Annie Minerva Turnbo Pope Malone was born in 1869 and died in 1957. She lived a very long and amazing life. Historically, her life covers two important periods in the civil rights movement of American blacks. Like Madam C.J. Walker, she was born into a world just recovering from the Civil War, when the passage of constitutional amendments began the long trail to equality for blacks. When she died in 1957, a new force was entering American politics, one which would culminate in the South in the 1960s. This force was the revitalized civil rights movement, which unyieldingly called for true enforcement of the rights guaranteed a hundred years before. The Voting Rights Act of 1964 was the keystone to that enforcement, and Annie Turnbo Malone lived almost long enough to see it. Because of this, she sometimes seems like a figure removed in history from Madam C. J. Walker, who died in 1919. But Annie Turnbo Malone's convictions and methods were the product of many of the same experiences as those that shaped Madam C.J. Walker.

Annie Turnbo Malone was born on August 9, 1869, in Metropolis, Illinois. She was raised in poverty on a farm there. Her parents were Robert Turnbo and Isabella Cook Turnbo. She was the tenth of eleven children.

Robert Turnbo fought for the cause of freedom in the Civil War in the Union army. His wife was forced to flee from Kentucky, where they had lived, with the first of her two children. Husband and wife were later reunited in Metropolis, Illinois, where the other children were born.

Like Madam Walker, Annie Turnbo Malone was orphaned young. Also like Madam C.J. Walker, her older siblings took over raising her. In Annie Turnbo's case, a sister brought her up, mostly in Peoria, Illinois.

Annie Turnbo Malone received more schooling than Madam C.J. Walker did. She attended public grade school in Metropolis, and then the public high school in Peoria. Later in her life, she received honorary degrees from Kittrell College and Western College. These degrees testified that she possessed the skills of Master of the Arts.

While still a young woman, Annie Turnbo Malone is said to have recognized the problem that many black women had in presenting a well-groomed appearance in American society. Black women in Peoria used oils, soap, and goose fat to try and straighten their hair, generally without hope for success. In the late 1890s, Annie Turnbo Malone began working with chemicals in an effort to find a better method than the oils, soaps, and goose fat.

One of the problems she faced was that current chemical solutions were dangerous. They damaged the hair follicles and the scalp,

When Madam Walker moved her business headquarters to Indianapolis, Indiana, as part of her plan to expand to a

national market, she bought a house at 540 North West Street. In this photo she is seen standing on the porch of the house.

causing painful and ugly burns. Black women took a risk when using these products, and there was a need for safer and more reliable methods.

In Lovejoy, Illinois, Annie Turnbo Malone worked out a solution to straightening hair and growing replacement locks. She is said by some to be the first to develop and patent a hot pressing iron and comb for straightening hair. She also sold door to door a product which she called Wonderful Hair Grower, as Madam C.J. Walker would later call her own product.

Annie Turnbo Malone and three assistants worked from door to door giving free hair and scalp treatments to prospective clients in order to convince them of their worth.

In 1902, she moved to St. Louis, Missouri, which may have been when Madam C.J. Walker worked for her, or at least came into her orbit. It is unlikely that Madam Walker was not influenced in some way by Annie Turnbo Malone's Poro Company. Claude Barnett, the Negro Associated Press founder and an advertising advisor to Poro College, claims that Madam C.J. Walker was a Poro trainee.

Poro itself was a word which meant an organization devoted to physical and spiritual self-discipline and improvement. It is West

African in origin. Annie Turnbo Malone intended her company to demonstrate the best that the black beauty culture could offer.

She opened her first Poro business in 1902 in St. Louis, Missouri. Her first headquarters were at 2223 Market Street. The World's Fair, a cavalcade of culture and the nation's achievements, was held in St. Louis in 1904. The World's Fair brought many people to St. Louis, and generally increased the prosperity of businesses there.

Before a year had passed, Poro Company was distributing products to black women all over the Midwest. Annie Turnbo Malone used some of the same marketing strategies that were so successful for Madam C.J. Walker. She advertised in black newspapers, which could be found in large northern cities, held press conferences to ensure that her products received publicity, and traveled through the South to promote her products. She also trained agents to sell her wares.

Her work was successful. By 1910, she could move to bigger rooms at 3100 Pine Street in St. Louis. It is possible that she, and not Madam Walker, was the first black self-made millionairess in the United States, but the zenith of her success was more likely in the 1920s, after Madam C.J. Walker's death.

Madam Walker selected Indianapolis, Indiana, as the headquarters for her company because it was centrally located

in the most populous area of the United States and because it had excellent rail facilities for transporting her products.

In 1917 or 1918 she started Poro College, which was similar to Lelia College. Poro College was a beauty training school. It was housed in an impressive complex, the Poro plant. The Poro plant was made up of the college, the Poro Annex building, and the Poro Garage building. The Poro plant contained equipment and furnishings valued at over a million dollars, a huge sum for the early twentieth century. The main building and the annex housed classrooms, laboratories, barber shops, an auditorium, a cafeteria, a dining room, an ice cream parlor, a bakery, a theater, and a roof garden.

By 1926, Poro may have had as many as 75,000 agents operating in the United States, the Caribbean, and other locations. There were 175 people working at Poro College training beauticians and agents.

By 1927, Poro College became the site of some very special philanthropy. A tornado hit St. Louis, leaving many people in dire need of relief. Thousands were sheltered, clothed, and fed at Poro College, which was a primary relief location for the Red Cross.

Annie Turnbo Malone's good works include far more than disaster relief in 1927. She contributed heavily to Negro education in many ways. She may have supported two full-time students at every black land-grant college in America. She contributed more than $25,000 to Howard University's Medical School. She gave large sums of money to Tuskegee Institute, to the St. Louis building campaign of the colored YWCA, and to black orphanages.

She served on the boards and committees of many beneficent organizations, including the board of directors of the St. Louis Colored Orphans Home, the Colored Women's Federated Clubs in St. Louis, and the National Negro Business League and the Committee on Interracial Cooperation.

She also gave generous gifts to her employees, including diamond rings for employees who had worked for her for five years, and gold to real estate investors. She also gave prizes for punctuality and attendance.

But Annie Turnbo Malone did not manage her wealth so that it would last throughout her lifetime. She died with only a hundred thousand dollars, where once she was worth a reported fourteen million.

Her financial problems were created by many factors. First, there were her marriages. She was briefly married to a Mr. Pope in 1903, but soon divorced him because he interfered with her developing business. Then she married Aaron Malone, the root of many of her financial woes.

Aaron Malone was president and chief manager of Poro Company until their much talked about divorce in 1927. Aaron Malone sued his wife for control of the company, relying on help from sources he had courted while still married. Malone demanded one-half of the business assets because he claimed that the success of the business was due to contacts he had made prior to the marriage.

Many famous black figures took sides, but the most powerful champion for Annie Turnbo Malone was Mary McLeod Bethune, then president of the National Association of Colored Women. Annie Turnbo Malone's philanthropic work stood her in good stead during this fight, and eventually the tide of opinion turned to her side. Aaron Malone received a settlement of $200,000, but Annie Turnbo Malone kept the business from going into receivership.

But the financial problems continued. A nuisance lawsuit, eventually dismissed, cost her money and some bad publicity. In 1937, another employee also claimed credit for her business' success, and the settlement forced the sale of the wonderful St. Louis property.

But the worst problem of all was Annie Turnbo Malone's failure to pay taxes. In the

1920s, all luxuries and cosmetics were taxed a twenty percent excise tax, which she refused to pay. She did not pay many of the taxes owing on her business and the government sued her frequently. By 1951, she owed so much in taxes that most of the Poro property was sold by the government.

Annie Turnbo Malone died of a stroke in Chicago, Illinois, in 1957.

Less is known about the other cosmetics entrepreneur and philanthropist, Sarah Spencer Washington.

Sarah Spencer Washington was born on June 6, 1889, in Berkeley, Virginia. Her parents were Joshua and Ellen Douglass Phillips. She was well educated, attending the public schools in Berkeley, and then the Lincoln Preparatory School in Philadelphia, Pennsylvania, and Norfolk Mission College in Norfolk, Virginia. She also studied beauty culture in York, Pennsylvania. Finally, she did advanced work in chemistry at Columbia University.

From 1905 to 1913, she worked as a dressmaker. Her family encouraged her to become a schoolteacher, but in 1913, she became a beauty culturist instead. She opened a small hairdressing operation in Atlantic City, New Jersey, that year. In the evenings, she went door to door with her products, much like

In marketing her products, Madam Walker made use of "before" and "after" illustrations. In this case the illustration is a series

of paintings showing the improvement resulting from use of her hair care products. Later photographs were used.

Madam C.J. Walker and Annie Turnbo Malone did.

By 1919, though, she was so successful that she founded her own company, the Apex Hair and News Company. Sarah Spencer Washington was sole owner and president of that operation. She eventually opened Apex colleges and beauty supply stations in New York and New Jersey.

Her greatest successes began in the 1930s, after the Poro empire and the Walker business were losing luster. From 1937 to 1939, Sarah Spencer Washington built laboratories in Atlantic City, New Jersey. More than seventy-five beauty products were manufactured there then. Today, more than two hundred Apex products are manufactured and packed there.

Again, phenomenal wealth could be harvested from meeting the needs of black female consumers. As many as five hundred people may be employed in eleven American Apex colleges, and there may have been as many as 35,000 or 45,000 Apex agents in the United States. Foreign schools and agents increase those figures.

In 1939, Sarah Spencer Washington received a medallion at the New York World's Fair, recognizing international success in the business world.

Like the other pioneers, Madam C.J. Walker and Annie Turnbo Malone, Sarah Spencer Washington used her success to help others. A notable story in this regard relates to her business motto. During the Great Depression of the United States in the 1920s and 1930s, she continued to rely on manual labor rather than on the machines that could increase her output and profits, because she wanted to provide steady employment for all of her workers. She said that Apex's slogan was "Now is the time to plan your future by learning a depression-proof business."

Sarah Spencer Washington, like Annie Turnbo Malone and Madam C.J. Walker, donated a great deal of money to black charities and educational institutes. She endowed a girls' home for the National Youth Administration Program and gave twenty acres of land as a camping ground for black children. She donated money for scholarships and charities yearly.

More than anything, love for their fellow human beings was a feature of all three women's lives. Their businesses were built on a perception of human need, and conducted with kindness.

Chapter Seven

Dreams, Riches, and War

BESIDES KNOWING THAT SHE had done her fellow human beings a tremendous service both by her example and by her generosity, there were wonderful material rewards for Madam C.J. Walker's successful business career. She worked hard and encouraged all other women to do the same, and in the last years of her life she played hard too. Madam Walker had earned a magnificent reward for her early years of toil and sacrifice: she was rich beyond most people's wildest dreams. The lavish ways in which she spent her wealth will long be remembered.

At the peak of her success, Madam Walker set an example for others, not only in her business dealings, but also in sharing her wealth through charitable contributions.

Most memorable of all is the house that she had built in New York. Many wealthy people, all white, lived in a community on the Hudson River in New York. In 1916, Madam C.J. Walker purchased a large plot of land on the eastern shore of the Hudson, a place called Irvington-on-the-Hudson. On that piece of land she built her dream house. Newspapers from the time make clear what an astonishing action Madam Walker had undertaken.

The *New York Times* said, "On her first visits to inspect her property, the villagers, noting her color, were puzzled, but when it became known she was the owner...they could only gasp in astonishment. *Impossible!* they exclaimed. *No woman of her race could own such a place.* To say that the village, when the report was verified, was surprised would be putting the case mildly. *Does she really intend to live there, or is she building it as a speculation?* the people asked."

Madam C.J. Walker really did intend to live there, and she did just that. She did not plan to use the property for speculation or to sell for a higher price to the next buyer, presumably white, who offered. Instead, Madam C.J. Walker in her private life was breaching the color bar that existed even for a wealthy black.

Madam Walker ignored the incredulity of her neighbors and the astonishment of local newspapers. Black newspapers encouraged her defiance of the unwritten laws of segregation.

Madam Walker was apparently successful in deflating any possible hostility arising from her home in Irvington-on-the-Hudson. Later it was said, "Mme. Walker's unassuming ways have kept down any possible friction that might have arisen due to her presence. Instead of dislike, her neighbors have learned to respect her."

For Madam Walker, her house was a symbol of all that she had accomplished, all that a black person could strive for. The ornate and expensive decorations, the parties with glittering guest lists, and the location smack in the middle of a formerly all-white enclave gave all blacks a symbol of pride, and of the reward that comes from hard work. All things were possible, even when a person began life in crippling poverty.

Madam Walker told the *New York Times,* "I was born forty-nine years ago, was married at fourteen, and was left a widow at twenty with a little girl to support. If I have accomplished anything in life, it is because I have been willing to work hard. I never yet started anything

Madam Walker loved automobiles. She owned one electric car and four gasoline-powered vehicles, and she used them for travel whenever possible. However, she had one harrowing

experience while traveling in Mississippi in 1916, when the automobile she was in barely missed being hit by a freight train at an unmarked crossing.

doubtingly, and I have always believed in keeping at things with a vim. When a little more than twelve years ago I was a washerwoman, I was considered a good washerwoman and laundress. I am proud of that fact. At times I also did cooking, but, work as I would, I seldom could make more than a dollar fifty a day. I got my start by giving myself a start. It is often the best way. I believe in push, and we must push ourselves."

Those are wise words indeed. From earning a dollar fifty a day, Madam Walker grew to be worth more than a million dollars by giving herself a push. She gained, in addition to money, a sense of self-respect that comes from knowing she had done her best and that she could depend on herself.

Ida B. Wells-Barnett, black journalist and anti-lynching activist, recalls Madam C.J. Walker's simple pride in what she had accomplished. "I asked her on one occasion what on earth she would do with a thirty-room house. She said, 'I want plenty of room in which to entertain my friends. I have worked so hard all my life that I would like to rest.'"

The mansion on the Hudson River was fabulous. It was a fantasy come true for Madam C.J. Walker and her circle of relatives and companions. The house, which cost her approximately $350,000, overlooked the river and the magnificent spectacle of the New Jersey Palisades. It was designed by the black architect Vertner W. Tandy and covered 113 feet by 60 feet. The house stood on four-and-a-half acres of prime real estate.

The house was christened "Lewaro" by one of Madam Walker's distinguished guests there, famous opera singer Enrico Caruso. He suggested "Lewaro" because it used the first letters of Madam Walker's daughter's name, Lelia Walker Robinson.

Madam Walker had, on her cream-colored mock-Georgian estate, a formal Italian garden and a swimming pool. She purchased for her entertainment a Weber piano and a Victrola covered in gold leaf, and an expensive Estey pipe organ. Years later, Lelia Walker Robinson's guests would be awakened to the sound of the pipe organ.

Other furnishings were equally impressive. She purchased Hepplewhite furniture, priceless, deep-piled rugs from Persia, and many large oil paintings. Rich, handmade tapestries covered the walls. Bronze and ivory statues lined the hall cabinets, and the dining room had hand-painted ceilings and recessed lighting. The libraries were full of rare books and American classics from the black author

Madam Walker built an elegant mansion on four-and-a-half acres beside the Hudson River in New York. Opera singer Enrico Caruso gave it the name "Lewaro," taking the first two

letters of the three parts of her daughter's name, Lelia Walker Robinson. The above photograph of the Villa Lewaro was taken during a Walker convention.

Paul Laurence Dunbar to Mark Twain. The staircase was a sweeping curve of white marble. Her bed was tented in red velvet and commanded a view of the river.

In the formal landscaped gardens, Madam Walker had prayer trees planted. The prayer trees were imported from Japan. They cost ten thousand dollars.

In addition to the pianos and organs and furniture, Madam C.J. Walker bought four automobiles and an electric car. The electric car was a coupe. The coupe could reach a speed of thirty miles per hour. It could go for thirty-five to fifty miles off one battery charge. Her nieces loved to ride around the neighborhood in one of Madam Walker's grand vehicles.

She enjoyed spending money and was generous to her family and friends. Madam Walker wrote to Freeman B. Ransom about one of her purchases, a fancy car for her daughter Lelia. "Am writing to let you know I have given a check for $1,381.50 to the Cadillac Motor Co. Won't you see to it that the check is cashed?...I guess you think I am crazy, but I had a chance to get just what Lelia wanted in a car."

Ransom wrote back, "No, I don't think you are crazy, but think you are very hard on your bank account. I take pleasure in the fact that there can hardly be anything else for you to buy, ha, ha!"

In addition to Villa Lewaro, Madam C.J. Walker was by now a substantial property owner. She shrewdly understood the value of real estate investments. Besides buying a large share of the 600 block in Indianapolis' Indiana Avenue, she bought lots in that city's Ballard and Hilltop areas. She purchased two houses in New York's Harlem, a place which attracted her greatly. In her later years, she would forsake living in the Midwest for the stimulating atmosphere of New York. The two houses that she purchased in Harlem between 1913 and 1915 were located at 108-110 West 136th Street. She converted this property into a beauty parlor and school after investing money in substantial remodeling.

Madam Walker was proud of her efforts on the Harlem holding. The parlor was redesigned until Madam Walker felt that blacks would look to it as a symbol of the gracious life that could be achieved by working hard. She added a bay window to the property and had a front of Indiana limestone added. The upstairs floors were used as living quarters. Booker T. Washington himself may have been a guest at the opening of the Harlem property.

Madam Walker bought many other pieces of

property. In the Bronx, New York, she purchased an apartment house at 374 Central Park West and a house at 1447-49 Boston Road. She also owned real estate in large urban centers, including Los Angeles, Chicago, Savannah, and St. Louis. In addition, she owned property in Idlewild, Michigan, and Gary, Indiana.

Real estate did not always come cheaply. She turned down, after lengthy consideration, a $300,000 apartment on New York's Riverside Drive. Despite this restraint, though, Madam Walker did strain herself a bit. Villa Lewaro was mortgaged and the gold leaf piano and the Estey pipe organ took some years to pay off.

There were excesses. In one afternoon, reportedly, Madam C.J. Walker spent seven thousand dollars on jewelry, a phenomenal sum in the years before World War I. She also over-ate, with detrimental effects on her health. Her social and working life were so hectic that doctors repeatedly ordered her to rest. She rarely heeded them, although she took one memorable vacation to Hot Springs in Arkansas.

The vacation was triggered by a near tragedy. She was traveling through Clarksdale, Mississippi, in November of 1916, when a terrifying thing happened. A'Lelia Perry Bundles quotes Madam Walker's letter to Freeman B. Ransom about the incident: "After leaving the church, we had to cross a railroad track. As soon as the car we were in got on the track we heard a man yelling, 'Get out of the way!' We looked around in time to see a freight train backing down on us, not a bell ringing or anything. The chauffeur in the nick of time put on more gas and shot forward. The train all but grazed the back of the car in which we were riding. I haven't been myself since."

The doctor whom Madam Walker saw after the train incident advised her to have not less than six weeks' rest. He told Madam Walker's traveling companion that Madam Walker was on the verge of a nervous collapse. Extracting promises from Ransom and the traveling companion to keep Madam Walker quiet for at least six weeks did little good, however. Madam Walker may have intended to be relaxed, but she was not idle by nature and had a hard time following the doctor's orders.

She wrote to Ransom from Hot Springs, Arkansas, "I promise you I am going to let all business alone and look strictly after my health except little things which I am going to write to you about now. Ha. Ha."

Hot Springs was a spa that catered to the wealthy. It possessed European bathhouses featuring hot mineral springs. Massages, herb teas and brisk water jets were available. The mineral springs were supposed to cure a variety of problems, including overwork. They were located by Ouachita National Forest, a tranquil spot in central Arkansas.

Lelia and Alice Kelly, one of Madam Walker's executives, joined Madam Walker at Hot Springs hoping to induce her to stay until she was fully recovered. They were frequently to be found at the bathhouse owned by the Knights of Pythias. The Knights of Pythias was a black fraternal group.

Madam Walker stayed at the luxurious Hot Springs retreat until February of 1917, returning to New York shortly before World War I broke out in April.

The war created a moral quandary for black leaders of American society. Did blacks want to serve and maybe die for a segregated America? Blacks were treated poorly in many parts of the country. The Ku Klux Klan was active. Nearly three thousand blacks were lynched between 1885 and 1916. White mobs murdered whole groups of blacks and went unpunished because states did not enforce anti-lynching laws adequately. Jim Crow laws flourished. Jim Crow laws were laws segregating and restricting blacks from doing things with white people, like sitting in the same theaters together. Blacks were not allowed to eat in the same restaurants as whites and were treated with a humiliating lack of respect for their basic human dignity.

Even wealthy blacks like Madam C.J. Walker were targets of discrimination. But she responded with spirit. Her self-respect and courage led her to fight many battles with segregation, including a notable one in Indianapolis.

Madam Walker loved going to the movies. She liked the work of comedian Charlie Chaplin and epic director Cecil B. DeMille. One night, she attended the Isis Theatre in Indianapolis and discovered that she was supposed to pay twenty-five cents for admission because she was black. Whites only paid a dime.

Madam Walker's attorney, Freeman B. Ransom, sued the theater on her behalf. His complaint accused the Isis of "unwarranted discrimination because of the color of this plaintiff." The case did not go far. No further records are public and the theater probably settled out of court.

But Madam Walker was not finished yet. She decided to expand her business in Indianapolis, creating the block-long Walker

Building, which was completed many years later, perhaps by Lelia Walker Robinson. The Walker Building, finished in 1928 at 617 Indiana Avenue, contained, in addition to the Walker Manufacturing Company, the Walker College of Beauty Culture, a beauty salon, a barber shop, a pharmacy, a grocery store, professional offices, and the Majestic Walker Theater. The Majestic Walker Theater catered to black moviegoers. The rest of the Walker complex was a safe harbor for black doctors, lawyers, musicians, businessmen, and patrons of the arts because Jim Crow laws prevented the use of white office buildings by black professionals.

Madam Walker, faced with the prejudice of white America, was nevertheless certain that black Americans should support the nation's war effort. The support of black soldiers might prove to the majority of the populace that blacks deserved full and equal citizenship in a country they were prepared to sacrifice even their lives for. Two leaders of the National Association for the Advancement of Colored People (NAACP), W.E.B. Du Bois and James Weldon Johnson, encouraged black support of the war effort. Walker approved of their stance. She used her name to bolster recruitment and visited training camps around the

A'Lelia Walker Robinson, after divorcing her husband, moved to New York in 1913 to open a second Lelia College. Her townhouse became the center of society during the Harlem Renaissance.

country. She advised black soldiers to be the best that they could.

But her efforts were betrayed. In the summer of 1917, race riots broke out across the nation, including the East St. Louis massacre. In that horrible event, thirty-nine black men, women, and children were murdered by a rioting mob. White policemen either watched or even participated.

Community leaders in Harlem responded to the outcry of blacks from across the nation. Madam Walker helped to organize the Negro Silent Protest Parade. It was held in Manhattan, New York, on July 28, 1917.

The march was funereal. Ten thousand blacks, dressed somberly, carrying signs protesting the Jim Crow laws, lynching, and the abrogation of voting rights, marched in silence as drums rolled. "Treat Us So That We May Love Our Country," the banners read. Walker agents formed part of the marchers.

Twenty thousand spectators approved the public show of solidarity. Walker's Harlem group continued their efforts to make lynching a federal crime in an effort to counter the inadequate state enforcement of state anti-lynching laws.

They wrote a petition to President Woodrow Wilson, whose record on race relations was so far neglectful. The petition expressed the views of such black community leaders as James Weldon Johnson and W. E. B. Du Bois of the NAACP, *New York Age* publisher Fred Moore, the Reverend Adam Clayton Powell, Sr., of Harlem's Abyssinian Baptist Church, and Harlem realtor John E. Nail.

President Wilson's secretary, Joseph Tumulty, made them an appointment with the President in order for them to present their petition. They went to Washington, D.C., and appeared at the White House as scheduled. They were informed that President Wilson would not see them as promised, as he was signing a bill related to feeding farm animals.

The President failed to keep faith with his campaign promises for a better America for the Negro. He treated the petitioners with an all too familiar discourtesy. But they kept trying.

Madam Walker, in her position as head of the Walker Company, led her agents to send a telegram to Woodrow Wilson protesting the lynching. And she continued to support the fight for civil rights and to impress upon her agents that they must fight, too.

"This is the greatest country under the sun," she told them. "But we must not let our love of country, our patriotic loyalty, cause us to abate one whit in our protest against wrong and injustice. We should protest until the American sense of justice is so aroused that such affairs as the East St. Louis riot be forever impossible."

Madam C.J. Walker's unflinching determination to create a world where black men and women could share in the dignity and wealth of equal opportunity caused her to become a symbol to many blacks in her time. Her fantastic house, her outspoken courage, her perseverance in the face of tremendous odds won her admiration and fame that persists to this day. She reminds us always to work hard, and never to give up hope.

Madam Walker agreed with James Weldon Johnson, noted poet and NAACP leader, who urged African Americans to serve in World War I to prove themselves worthy of full rights at home.

Chapter Eight

Fulfilling a Need

MADAM C.J. WALKER understood how hard the struggle to achieve can sometimes be. She was poor most of her life and had to overcome many tremendous obstacles. She raised a daughter alone and educated that daughter well. She did it during a time when most blacks had few places where they could go for a helping hand. Madam Walker had to become her own helping hand, and later she would reach out and help other blacks, too.

One of her most heartwarming victories is against illiteracy. Madam Walker was the child

Madam Walker planned to attend the Pan African Congress in Paris organized by W.E.B. Du Bois in conjunction with the Versailles Peace Conference, but the U.S. government refused her a passport.

of former slaves. She was raised in the Reconstruction South, where going to school was impossible due to economics and due to the violence that spread like an ugly stain through many of the post-Civil War states. Because of her background, Madam Walker did not have a chance to read and write. But she went to night school after long days at the washtub. And then, after she had become a businesswoman, prosperous beyond all dreams, she was able to hire tutors to teach her to read and write. She surrounded herself with intelligent and well-educated people, the cream of the black community of her time. Educators like Booker T. Washington and Mary McLeod Bethune were her friends.

Reportedly, at the beginning of her business, she wrote her name so illegibly on checks and bank documents that it was known to all of the bank employees that she was functionally illiterate. But she worked hard at learning to read and write, as she did at everything she had done—cooking, washing, and finally hair care product sales. Eventually, her script was so clear and legible that the bank called her to find out if the new handwriting on the checks and bank documents was really hers. What a moment of triumph that must have been!

With her newfound abilities, Madam C.J. Walker began to read extensively. She especially enjoyed American literature and history, in which she became well versed.

The parties and musicals and balls that she gave in her Irvington-on-the-Hudson mansion were thronged with the famous and distinguished. The first official guests entertained at the Villa Lewaro make up an impressive list. That list includes Emmett J. Scott, Booker T. Washington's former secretary, then of the National Negro Business League; Dean William Pickens of Morgan College; Charlotte Hawkins Brown, the founder of the Palmer Memorial Institute; Ida Wells-Barnett and fellow political activist A. Phillip Randolph; Fred Moore, publisher of the *New York Age;* Robert Sengstacke Abbott, publisher of the *Chicago Defender;* scholar Arthur Schomburg; Maggie Lena Walker, a banker; Margaret Murray Washington; composer Harry T. Burleigh; Henry Watson Furniss, former minister to Haiti; NAACP executives John Hurst, Walter White, and James Weldon Johnson; the poet William Stanley Braithwaite; and Carter G. Woodson, who founded the Association for the Study of Negro Life and History.

She was well liked by her famous company.

Madam Walker was outspoken in her opposition to the increasing number of race riots and lynchings of blacks throughout the United States in the first two decades of the twentieth century.

She helped to organize the Silent March down New York's Fifth Avenue in 1917 to protest the lynchings, and in her will she left $5,000 to the NAACP's anti-lynching fund.

She was noted for her generosity and made friends wherever she went. It became usual for her to be honored at public events. For example, when she attended a basketball game at the Manhattan Casino on Christmas night 1918, she received an ovation at her entrance and was requested to throw the ball from her box. The mayor of New York City himself invited her to go out on his boat to observe the return of the Atlantic fleet from the war.

There were many reasons she was so honored. For example, the National Association of Colored Women led a fund drive to pay off the mortgage on abolitionist Frederick Douglass' home in Cedar Hill, Washington, D.C. Madam C.J. Walker was the greatest individual contributor, having given five hundred dollars, and the NACW wanted to thank her. They invited her to their annual convention in Denver, Colorado. The ceremony included the ritual burning of the mortgage. NACW President Mary B. Talbert and Madam C.J. Walker set the document alight while the audience sang "Hallelujah, 'Tis Done." Then the crowd rose to its feet in ovation. Madam Walker had helped to preserve yet another symbol of success for her people.

Before her death in 1919, Madam Walker donated five thousand dollars to the NAACP's anti-lynching fund. It was the largest gift received by the organization to date. The donation was announced at the NAACP's Anti-Lynching Conference at Carnegie Hall in Manhattan, New York. The 2,500 delegates greeted the news with a standing ovation. Other delegates were so inspired by the pledge that they poured in offers of their own. An Arkansas farmer promised one thousand dollars on the spot. An additional $3,400 was forthcoming from pledges that week.

She was known to have given many generous donations to institutes that helped black men, women, and children. For example, she donated five thousand dollars to her friend Mary McLeod Bethune's Florida school, the Daytona Normal and Industrial Institute for Negro Girls. She left five thousand dollars to Lucy Laney's Haines Institute in Augusta, Georgia. She sponsored a teacher at the Palmer Memorial Institute, a black preparatory school in Sedalia, North Carolina, founded by Charlotte Hawkins Brown.

Madam Walker emphasized education and self-help. She offered her own employees, the thousands and thousands of loyal Walker agents, a future that did not include low-paid, demanding domestic work. She taught her customers to bring out the best in their personal appearance so that they could go anywhere with dignity and a sense of self-worth. She gave large sums of money to educate Negro professionals.

As a political activist, she was not afraid to voice her opinions. She supported the National Equal Rights League, an organization run by Monroe Trotter. Her own advisors were worried about this radical move because, as a businesswoman, she might face many repercussions from the agencies that regulated businesses. William Monroe Trotter's NERL was one of the groups that planned a peace conference in Paris at the end of World War I. Peace negotiations between Germany and the United States, Great Britain, France, Italy, and Japan were underway in Paris. Trotter, Walker, and many black intellectuals and activists were duly worried that the official negotiations would ignore the needs of black Americans as well as blacks in the African colonies owned by various European countries. Consequently, the NERL and a group called the Pan-African Congress organized by W.E.B. Du Bois, created an alternative conference in Paris.

Ida Wells-Barnett and Madam C.J. Walker were among the delegates elected to attend the proposed Trotter-Du Bois conference in

Among the earliest guests Madam Walker entertained at the Villa Lewaro was the noted educator Ida B. Wells-Barnett, with whom she planned to attend the Versailles Peace Conference.

Paris. Freeman B. Ransom worried about the radical association on Madam Walker's part because he felt that she had more to lose should the government decide the NERL was subversive.

Madam Walker decided to go anyway. Unfortunately, Trotter was denied a passport by the State Department, as was Madam Walker and other of the expected delegates. They could not go to Paris. Du Bois' Pan-African Congress still met there but could not prevail upon the official treaty makers to guarantee equality or civil rights for blacks throughout the world.

Madam Walker was also, for a short time, part of the group that formed the International League of the Darker Peoples in early 1919. Adam Clayton Powell, Sr., was the primary founder of this organization that aimed to promote the rights and interests of people of color throughout the world.

Madam Walker was criticized for her courage in opposing inequality. Colonel William Jay Schieffelin, treasurer of the Welfare League of a black infantry unit, wanted her to moderate her pressure for equal treatment of black veterans. She, in turn, criticized his approach sharply and continued to speak on behalf of the returning soldiers.

For her efforts on their behalf both before and after the war, she was remembered by many black soldiers with affection and gratitude.

Early in her business career, Madam Walker had learned to fight for her own rights. At first, even with her impressive business record, she was a victim of sexism from the men who would later greet her with respect. An incident that she recalled with some force was the 1912 National Negro Business League convention. Booker T. Washington and the other leaders of the conference did not want to let a woman speak. But Madam Walker, as ever, supplied her own push and achieved her goal of recognition.

As Washington praised a male Negro banker for his work, she stalked up to the podium and seized the floor. She told the assembled audience, "I am a woman who came from the cotton fields of the South. I was promoted from there to a washtub. Then I was promoted to the cook kitchen, and from there I PROMOTED MYSELF into the business of manufacturing hair goods and preparations.... I have built my own factory on my own ground."

Her words of inspiration were so well received that she was asked to be a presenter at the 1913 convention. In 1914, she again addressed the National Negro Business League convention that was held in Muskogee, Oklahoma. She had words specifically for the women who were attending the conference.

"I am not merely satisfied in making money for myself, for I am endeavoring to provide employment for hundreds of the women of my race. I had little or no opportunity when I started out in life, having been left an orphan.... I had to make my own living and my own opportunity! But I made it! That is why I want to say to every Negro woman present, don't sit down and wait for the opportunities to come!...Get up and make them!" she told the convention.

Her newspaper advertisements for her Walker system expressed her best counsel: "Open your own shop. Secure prosperity and freedom. Many women of all ages confronted with the problem of earning a livelihood have mastered the Walker System."

She emphasized freedom from the chains of race and freedom from the chains of gender. Black women had a champion in Madam C.J. Walker. She was a product of the same experiences and could understand the desperate yearning for a better life. But she did not forget the men, either.

She conducted her business so as to employ

the largest number of blacks that she could. She constructed a group of houses for her Indianapolis workers in 1916, employing more blacks to do the building work. She explained her logic to a reporter.

"My business is largely supported by my own people, so why shouldn't I spend my money so that it will go back into colored homes? By giving my work to colored men, they are thus able to employ others, and if not directly, indirectly I am creating more jobs for our boys and girls."

For her 1917 Philadelphia convention of the Madam C.J. Walker Hair Culturists Union of America, she stressed two things: perseverance and Women's Duty to Women. She reminded her agents of their responsibility to others and encouraged them through their Walker service clubs to donate frequently and generously to the advancement of others in the community.

Her business ethos is therefore an example to everyone of the best that a community can offer: responsible, caring service that elevates more than the seller. She did not view her customers as victims to be milked for profits. Instead, she encouraged her agents to understand the circumstances under which many of their customers lived. Walker agents cus-

From the earliest days of her business success, Madam Walker shared her wealth by contributing to worthy causes. Here she is seen at the dedication of the black YMCA in Indianapolis in

1913. In the center, to her left, is Booker T. Washington, and directly behind her is Freeman B. Ransom. At the right in the rear is her doctor, Colonel Joseph Ward.

tomarily tried to encourage customers to take beauty treatments. However, many black women couldn't afford them. Madam Walker did not approve of abandoning these poor women to search for bigger game.

A'Lelia Perry Bundles reports that Madam Walker told her agents, "Do not be narrow and selfish to the extent that you would not sell goods to anyone because they do not take treatment from you. We are anxious to help all humanity, the poor as well as the rich, especially those of our race."

She also provided the more practical service of convincing black entrepreneurs that they could get their businesses off the ground despite the lack of funding or capital available more easily to white businesses. She emphasized the need for blacks to work together to provide community resources. And she demonstrated very forcefully how, by investing her profits in her own company repeatedly while the business was young, and by tireless efforts at self-promotion, she slowly built up a business that eventually returned over a million dollars. Others could do what she had done. Her message was clear.

Among Madam Walker's good friends were labor leader A. Philip Randolph and his wife Lucile, seen above, who opened a Walker salon in Harlem in 1913, giving up her job as a teacher.

Chapter Nine

Perseverance Was Her Motto

MADAM C.J. WALKER led an extraordinary life. In her later years she was rewarded richly for the many things that she had done for herself and others. But it was hard to be black and successful in the era in which she lived. Madam Walker was subject to stress and fatigue, which she at first ignored. She was not being careless in a way that is difficult to understand. She simply expected, all of her life, to put in an exhausting physical effort in order to simply exist.

As a child in a sharecropper's cabin in Louisiana, there was little time for illness. In order

In her will, Madam Walker left legacies to a number of African-American schools and colleges, among them Booker T. Washington's Tuskegee Institute.

to survive, even a child had to work from sunup to sundown. When a child or parent fell ill, there was no medical help available. Often the sick or injured person had to carry on working until he dropped. If one person could not work, others had to take on an additional burden. These terrible circumstances did not encourage black workers to rest until they had recovered.

There were so many hazards that people faced a hundred years ago that we will never experience ourselves. The threat of illness when there were no vaccines and antibiotics was huge. Illnesses that we expect to recover from were sometimes fatal. It was easy to die of influenza in Louisiana's damp, marshy river regions. Insects bred diseases such as malaria. Work accidents occurred, maiming and killing the unlucky.

In addition, chronic malnutrition caused far worse than hair loss. It weakened bodies causing the immune system to be less effective in fighting off illness. Surviving from day to day was a triumph for children such as Madam Walker once was.

A woman who, in her childhood, had seen death and tragedy so frequently would not view it in the same way that we do now. Madam Walker would not expect to live forever. She would not expect to live, perhaps, as long as the wealthier white people she knew in childhood. Death was an event that was accepted with more fatalism than we commonly possess. People did not take as many steps to prevent it as we commonly do now.

In addition, Madam Walker may have considered herself, rightly, to be strong in body because she had survived a childhood and young adulthood that had claimed the lives of her parents and brother at a fairly young age. She may have expected that strength to continue in the same unquestioning way it had when she was younger.

Her religious faith was also strong. She probably believed that whatever time God chose to take her from the earth, that was the correct time to go.

She made preparations for the dispensation of her worldly goods in the event that she died while still reasonably young. She even sought the advice of doctors when she first began to feel fatigued, perhaps as early as 1916. But she did not do all of the things that would have prevented her death at the age of fifty-one in 1919.

In 1916, after many exhausting sales trips, Madam Walker began to talk about shifting some of the burden to her assistants. On each

One of the important organizations Madam Walker supported, financially as well as vocally, was the National Association of

Colored Women, led by Mary McLeod Bethune, seen second from left in this photograph of the organization's officers in the 1940s.

long swing through a section of the United States, Madam Walker was acting as sales agent, speechmaker, and demonstrator. In addition, she was taking orders for her many beauty culture products.

The work was tiring. Madam Walker had always been an energetic woman, but in 1916 she told her executives that her sales trip through the South would be her last. It was on this trip that the train nearly ran over her car. She was persuaded to take the rest at Hot Springs, Arkansas, until February. The doctor whom she saw did not think it was long enough. He warned her that her blood pressure was too high. He warned her that she ate too much and ate the wrong foods. He warned her that she was under too much stress.

High blood pressure is a terrible disease. Unfairly, it affects blacks far more than it does people of other colors. Traditionally, the unhealthy high-fat diets of the South have been incorporated into many black homes. Stress levels are high for the economically disadvantaged. Even now, a black man is many more times likely to die from the results of high blood pressure than a white man is. High blood pressure needs to be monitored by a physician because it can lead to a fatal stroke or to diseases of the organs such as kidney failure. Unfortunately, physicians in Madam Walker's time did not have medication to lower high blood pressure as they have now.

To survive this dangerous and insidious disease, Madam Walker needed to change her lifestyle entirely. She needed to relax. She needed to be careful what she ate, and she needed to exercise. But it was not fashionable for women of her time to exercise. They did not understand the link between exercise and a healthy body in the same way that we do now.

But Madam Walker only stayed at Hot Springs in Arkansas until February of 1917. Then, because she felt so much better, she may have assumed that her high blood pressure had abated. But it had not. It is a disease that needs constant monitoring.

She returned to making sales trips, despite what she had said previously. She went on a two-month-long sales trip through Louisiana and Texas. Her business boomed, which meant that she had a lot more work to keep her busy.

Then Madam Walker threw herself into the design and building of Villa Lewaro. When her princely mansion was built, she began to throw parties to launch it into society. She was busy both with her business and with her social life, although she told Ida Wells-Barnett that she had worked so hard all of her life, she wanted the house as a place to rest.

Madam Walker had many servants to look after Villa Lewaro, but she did not relax as her doctors hoped. She thought that it would be pleasant to work in her garden, but of course she brought her famous perseverance and stubbornness to the task. She rose at six in the morning to work planting fruit and vegetables, weeding, and harvesting her crops. She said that "we are putting up fruit and vegetables by the wholesale." Even when she was supposed to be at rest, Madam Walker drove herself to work hard and to produce visible results.

Her blood pressure rose drastically in late 1917. Worried, her doctor sent her to a medical clinic and sanitarium to rest. It was located in Battle Creek, Michigan. But Madam Walker did not stay there long.

And when she left Battle Creek Sanitorium, she went to Des Moines, Iowa, instead of home to Villa Lewaro.

Madam Walker had received a coveted invitation to speak at a fund-raising dinner for the NAACP. She was obviously ill during this trip. A'Lelia Perry Bundles reports that George Woodson, the attorney who led her to make the speech to the NAACP dinner, was concerned for her health. He wrote to Freeman B. Ransom that he was so worried about Madam Walker's health that he took her pulse in the reception room after the meeting. He could tell that she was ill, but he could not persuade her to leave the cause or the people that she loved.

Madam Walker continued to make appearances at fund raisers for the NAACP. Her travels included Chicago, Indianapolis, Columbus (Ohio), and Pittsburgh. She was enraptured with the ovations and applause with which her audiences greeted her. She was beloved for her courage and for her generosity.

Madam Walker was also heavily involved in promoting the war effort. When the war ended on November 11, 1918, she became active in helping to improve the lives of returning black veterans and in fighting for their civil rights. There was little time on her agenda for the needed rest.

In early 1919, Madam Walker introduced five new products to her line. Business boomed. Profits expanded. Madam Walker worked harder. Her blood pressure rose.

Her doctor, Colonel Joseph Ward, became so alarmed that he ordered her to quit her day-to-day work for the Walker Company. Madam Walker tried to comply but, as always, she failed to let go of all that she needed to. She did not visit her office as much, but then she spent more time on her political activism. She regularly communicated with her offices and did much of the long-term planning for her holdings.

She stayed home at Villa Lewaro for a little while, but eventually she received a request that she decided not to pass up. Jessie Robinson, the wife of newspaper publisher C.K. Robinson and a one-time Walker agent, wanted Madam Walker to travel to St. Louis. Once there, Madam Walker was to launch the five new products that her company had unveiled.

Madam Walker was already unwell. She had a bad cold and was in a weakened condition. Once she arrived in St. Louis, her hostess became alarmed at how sick Walker had become. The Robinsons were asked by Walker to send her home to New York in a private railroad car. Their doctor and a nurse went with Madam Walker on the train, which was the fastest that 1919 had to offer. It was called the Twentieth Century Limited. Madam Walker's railway car was filled with flowers and excited great interest in her fellow passengers.

On arriving at the Villa Lewaro, Colonel

Joseph Ward examined Madam Walker. He was greatly saddened to realize that she would not survive this illness. Her high blood pressure had caused kidney disease, known as nephritis.

Madam Walker received the news with dignity. Then she made a codicil to her will. In that codicil, she again showed her tremendous selfless concern for others. She made a list of all the causes to which she wanted her money given generously. The five thousand dollars given to the NAACP anti-lynching fund, for example, was part of this bequest.

Madam Walker's codicil made it clear that she intended to leave $25,000 to deserving black causes. In fact, she left much more. She summoned Freeman B. Ransom. Lelia was traveling in Central America with her adopted daughter, Mae.

Madam Walker, while dying, received the news of Lelia's engagement to Dr. James Arthur Kennedy, an associate of Colonel Joseph Ward. This news pleased Madam Walker. Kennedy had just received a medal for his service in World War I. Madam Walker approved of the match. But before she finally married Kennedy in 1924, A'Lelia would marry Wiley Wilson, whom she would divorce in 1924. Within a few days, Madam Walker slipped into a coma from which she did not awaken. She died on May 25, 1919. Madam C.J. Walker was only fifty-one years old.

Her death caused great sorrow, as her life had caused great hope and joy. Lelia returned home from Panama, grief-stricken. Over one thousand mourners shared her sorrow at Madam Walker's funeral.

Madam Walker's pastor at the Mother Zion African Methodist Episcopal Zion Church of New York performed the services for her. The Twenty-third Psalm, Madam Walker's favorite, was read, and Madam Walker was covered in roses and buried at Woodlawn cemetery.

Many of her famous friends and admirers commented on her passing. Mary McLeod Bethune praised her as an inspiration to more than just blacks. Madam Walker had a lesson for the entire world.

W.E.B. Du Bois and journalist George Samuel Schuyler paid her tribute, as did so many others who had known and at times worked with her. Madam Walker would be missed terribly by all of the people whose lives she had touched and transformed.

Her will was complex. Lelia, by now called A'Lelia, was the executrix. There were four types of bequests. A'Lelia received the most important parts, including the Harlem holdings, Villa Lewaro, all of the personal property of Madam C.J. Walker, and a one-third interest in the Walker Company.

The next type of bequest concerned the remaining two-thirds of the company stock, which was bequeathed to five trustees, including A'Lelia again, and company attorney and long-time advisor Freeman B. Ransom.

The income from the stock was to be employed in the upkeep of Villa Lewaro and for the maintenance of the charities that Madam Walker named.

Over $100,000 was left outright to different charities, including the Home for Aged and Infirm Colored People in Pittsburgh, Pennsylvania, the Colored Orphans Home in St. Louis, The Haines Institute in Georgia, the educational establishment for blacks called Tuskegee Institute, and the NAACP. She even left $100,000 to found an academy in West Africa for indigent black girls.

Personal bequests made up the fourth type of inheritance. These personal bequests included money and special items for friends, other relatives, servants, and company employees. Her generosity was long remembered.

This complex will was not fully untangled and administered until 1926. The will itself was somewhat vague, and the problem of estate taxes and federal taxes took a long time to resolve. The federal estate tax in 1922 was paid on a total estate value of $509,864.

Madam Walker left far more than money, though, on her passing. She left the remembered knowledge of generosity and perseverance, energy and compassion. She left hope for all of the sales agents and salon workers who otherwise would have to become domestic servants. She left a call for a world in which the civil rights of everyone, black or white, were of equal importance. She left the women of her race knowing that they could create opportunities for themselves and follow their own dreams.

Her life touched so many others in its fifty-one years that it is hard to recall just one special occasion when she rose to greatness. She did it so many times. And she told us that we can do it, too.

After the end of World War I, Madam Walker worked hard to try to see that returning African-American veterans received the rights and recognition they deserved for their military service.

Chapter Ten

Unfinished Business

THE COMPANY THAT MADAM Walker founded is still in existence today. The work of this extraordinary woman lived on well past her death in 1919. But in many ways, she was the vital force behind the idea of beauty culture, and the business that she left unfinished was difficult to knit together by just one person.

Her daughter, A'Lelia Walker Robinson Kennedy, became the president of the Madam C.J. Walker Manufacturing Company. Freeman B. Ransom, as before, was the company attorney and manager.

During the Harlem Renaissance, A'Lelia, Madam Walker's daughter and successor as head of the Walker Company, became a patron of the arts. Entertainer Alberta Hunter was one of her good friends.

Ransom's position was familiar to him. For many years he had been Madam Walker's trusted right-hand man. He oversaw many business decisions and looked after her interests scrupulously while Madam Walker was on the road. She addressed much of her correspondence to him. It rings with a respect that never allowed them to address each other familiarly by first names, but the degree of trust and affection bestowed on Ransom was obviously considerable.

Robinson continued in his capacity as attorney, but his duties as manager were suddenly much enlarged. He was responsible for the actual management of the Walker company, although the profits were directly paid to A'Lelia and to the estate.

At first, A'Lelia had been a tremendous help in her mother's business. From the very early years, A'Lelia was the major assistant in her mother's business. She was literate before her mother could read and write. It was to A'Lelia that Madam C.J. Walker turned when she began running her mail-order business in 1906 Pittsburgh. Lelia College was overseen by Madam Walker's daughter, as was Lelia College in New York.

In the 1920s, A'Lelia showed great interest in the development of the Walker property in

Indianapolis, where the tremendous complex envisioned by her mother after the incident with the Isis Theatre had been built. This conglomerate of shops and professional offices may have been erected by A'Lelia rather than Madam C.J. Walker herself. They were completed in 1927 or 1928, well after Madam Walker's death in 1919.

The 1920s were a time of personal development for A'Lelia. She was a patron of the arts in Harlem, a largely black section of New York. Harlem was undergoing an explosion of artistic and intellectual growth in the 1920s. This explosion came to be known as the Harlem Renaissance.

Black poets such as Langston Hughes and Countee Cullen were familiar figures in the Harlem Renaissance, as were intellectuals such as W.E.B. Du Bois. Entertainers such as Alberta Hunter and the opera singer Enrico Caruso could be found in Harlem. Caruso, a white, was not alone in his attraction to this lively cultural gathering point. European royalty even visited the nightlife of Harlem.

In this colorful milieu, A'Lelia stood out like a princess. She was a tall and regal woman, and she dressed lavishly. Her nearly six feet in height was often topped with jeweled and feathered turbans. Her Harlem townhouse on

136th Street was remodeled. She christened it "The Dark Tower" after a poem by Countee Cullen. She also spent time at an apartment in New York's "Sugar Hill" district, 80 Edgecombe Avenue.

The Dark Tower, however, was her favorite place for entertaining the "glitterati" of Harlem. She had a special party room decorated with French gold wallpaper and red furniture, which could hold a hundred people. Generally, she invited a lot more. The poet Langston Hughes tells an amusing story about the crush at A'Lelia's parties, where a Scandinavian prince could not gain admission through the crowds.

"Word was sent in to A'Lelia Walker that His Highness, the Prince, was waiting without. A'Lelia sent back word that she saw no way of getting His Highness in, either, nor could she get herself out to greet him. But she offered to send refreshments downstairs to the Prince's car," Hughes wrote in *The Big Sea: An Autobiography* (1940).

Harlem was a thriving and wealthy place for blacks in the roaring twenties, unlike the sad and poverty-stricken associations it maintains today. Negro churchmen, doctors, lawyers, dentists, and pharmacists were among the professionals who chose to live and practice there. Hospitals, libraries, hotels, theaters, newspapers, and a shopping district, all for blacks, could be found within its two square miles. It was the home to poets, artists, writers, scholars, and political activists. The largest concentration of blacks in the United States lived and worked there. They would have been shocked to see it as a slum.

In 1923, A'Lelia made a splash in the society columns by throwing a lavish wedding, costing nearly forty thousand dollars, for her adopted daughter, Mae. The wedding was held at St. Philip's Episcopal Church in Harlem. It was christened the "million dollar wedding."

Although she retained the title to Villa Lewaro, the mansion in Irvington-on-the-Hudson was her mother's place more than A'Lelia's in spirit. A'Lelia enjoyed visits and house parties to the Villa Lewaro, but she preferred the more stimulating and lively atmosphere of Harlem.

After A'Lelia's death, Madam C.J. Walker had intended for the Villa Lewaro to be inherited by the NAACP. But at the end of the 1920s, the United States entered a period of severe economic depression that lasted until World War II, and the NAACP could not afford the upkeep. The mansion was sold eventually, with the NAACP receiving the proceeds from the sale in order that it might continue its work in promoting civil rights. Madam Walker was proud of the courageous efforts of the members of the NAACP.

A'Lelia was as generous and lavish in her spending as her mother had been. She was not a tireless businesswoman, however. As the 1920s wore on, A'Lelia spent less time with the business and more with her travels and her patronages in Harlem. The spirit of the Harlem Renaissance lived in A'Lelia.

Freeman B. Ransom took on the running of the Madam C.J. Walker Manufacturing Company as A'Lelia spent more time on her other activities. But, as he had with Madam Walker, he had trouble curbing A'Lelia's expenditures. A'Lelia eventually spent her share of profits from the manufacturing company. In addition, she mortgaged the New York beauty parlor, and accumulated many large debts. She even had to pawn her jewels.

The Walker Building which A'Lelia oversaw in Indianapolis was erected during the prosperity of the earlier 1920s, and A'Lelia financed it by taking out first and second mortgages on the Indiana property. She did not foresee the Great Depression that accompanied the stock market crash in 1929.

Sales dropped at the Walker building from

$595,000 to $130,000. By 1933, sales were at only $48,000. Blacks were hardest hit by all of the depression, and there was no money to be spent on luxuries such as beauty salons and the Majestic Walker Theater.

Other Walker businesses were also not depression-proof. The Harlem beauty parlor and another one in Pittsburgh had to be closed down. The Harlem building was leased to the City of New York in an effort to save the Walker holdings from creditors.

Long-running problems with the payment of back taxes also cast a pall over the economic future of the Walker properties, as did the cost of upkeep at Villa Lewaro.

Approximately thirteen thousand dollars per year was needed to maintain the mansion, and cash was no longer easy to obtain in the depression. The Villa Lewaro could not be easily sold because it was willed to the NAACP. The furnishings of the villa could be sold, however, and in 1930 that step was taken.

Sadly, the expensive furnishings, the antiques, the paintings, the tapestries and organ and statues raised only the unbelievable sum of fifteen hundred dollars.

A'Lelia herself fell prey to the same disease as her mother, high blood pressure. She died unexpectedly in August of 1931, after having

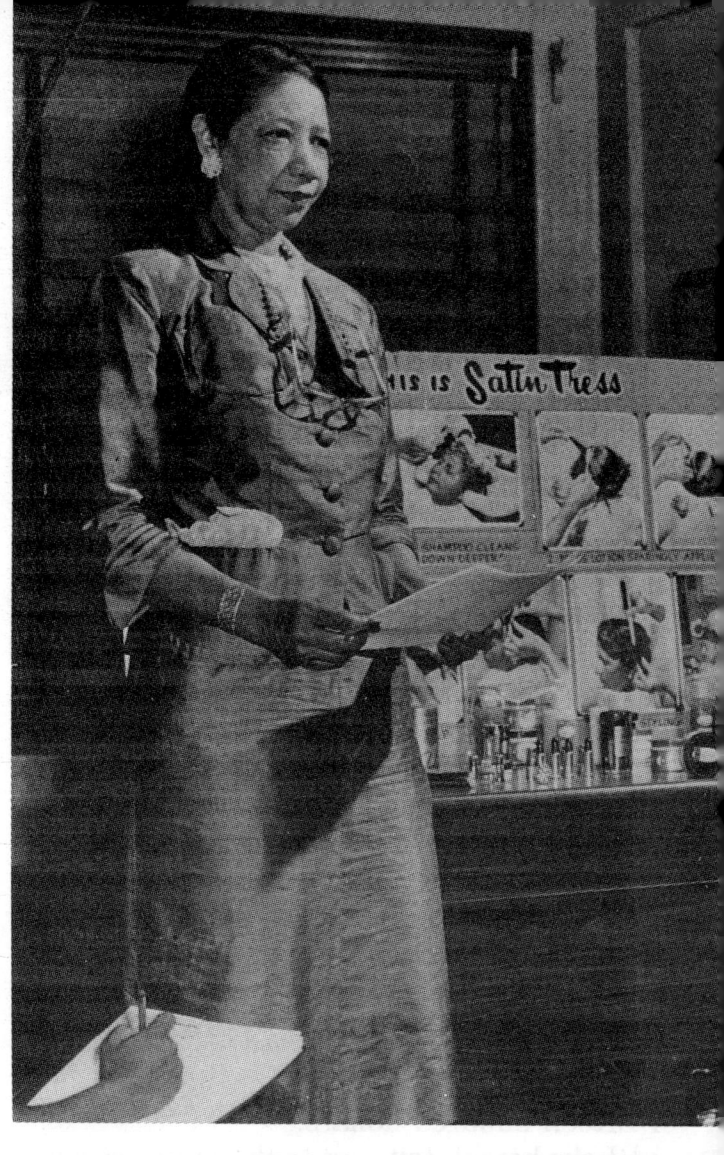

Violet Reynolds, seen here before a movie camera making an early commercial, was Madam Walker's trusted private secretary

for many years, and she continued to work for the Walker Company long after her mentor's death.

a stroke at the home of friends in Long Branch, New Jersey. She was only forty-six.

A'Lelia's funeral demonstrated how beloved she had been, in her turn. The Reverend Adam Clayton Powell, Sr., long-time friend of Madam Walker and then of her daughter, read the eulogy in a funeral parlor on Seventh Avenue in Harlem. Langston Hughes, speaking of the spirit shown at the funeral, which he thought would have pleased A'Lelia very much, said "It was a grand funeral and very much like a party." The music was swinging, and Mary McLeod Bethune, also a friend of A'Lelia's mother, spoke. Langston Hughes himself read a poem, "To A'Lelia." Girls from the Walker shops throughout the United States brought flowers to the funeral. Altogether, it was a very special farewell, and A'Lelia seemed to communicate that she was the "Joy Goddess" of Harlem in death as in life. She wanted no grieving. The Walkers were committed to wringing the best out of life, and that was what they had done.

The company passed through various hands of female relatives, as Madam C.J. Walker had wanted her company to always have a woman in the role of president. It had been her lifelong ambition to raise the status of women, to give them responsibility and the ability to govern their own lives. Her company had been instrumental in giving work and hope to thousands and thousands of black women who were her agents and customers during some of the most difficult parts of American history.

Madam C.J. Walker herself was a pioneer, both in the hair care business and in her personal conviction that women of all races deserve dignity and respect. She used her own hands to create a world where those qualities flourished, inside her hair care salons and in her theater and in her stately mansion.

Her legacy is even now being revitalized. The Walker Company in Indianapolis still manufactures her products, along with new lines. Sales continue, although advertising and promotion were not priorities for too long. The company is awaiting an overhaul, as were the buildings known as the Walker complex. In 1988, they were remodeled as part of the urban renewal of downtown Indianapolis. The Walker complex is a state historical landmark and is listed on the National Register of Historic Places. Its new name is the Madam Walker Urban Life Center.

Madam Walker would be pleased by the continuity of her work. She believed in perseverance and generosity, and she lived her beliefs. More could not be said of anyone.

INDEX

Abbott, Robert Sengstacke, 145
Abyssinian Baptist Church, 139
Ash, Mary Kay, 84
Association for the Study of
 Negro Life and History, 145
Atlantic City, New Jersey,
 115, 118
Augusta, Georgia, 149
Avon Company, 84

Barnett, Claude, 108
Battle Creek Sanitorium, 168
Berkeley, Virginia, 115
Bethune, Mary McLeod, 93–94,
 114, 144, 149, 172, 186
Braithwaite, William Stanley, 145
Breedlove, Alex (brother), 38, 67
Breedlove, Anjetta (niece), 78
Breedlove, Gladis (niece), 78
Breedlove, Louvenia (sister);
 see Powell, Louvenia
 Breedlove
Breedlove, Matti (niece), 78
Breedlove, Minerva (mother),
 25, 28, 34, 38
Breedlove, Owen (father), 25,
 28, 34–35, 38
Breedlove, Sarah; *see* Walker,
 Madam C.J.
Breedlove, Thirsapen (niece), 78
Brown, Charlotte Hawkins,
 145, 149
Bundles, A'Lelia Perry (great-
 great granddaughter), 63, 72,
 132, 158, 168
Burleigh, Harry T., 145
Burney family plantation, 23
Burney, Robert W., 25

Caruso, Enrico, 127, 179
Chaplin, Charlie, 135
Chicago Defender
 (publication), 145

Chicago, Illinois, 115, 132
Civil War, 10–11, 29, 35, 48,
 52, 104
Clark University, 49
Clarksdale, Mississippi, 132
Colfax Massacre, 34
Colorado Statesman
 (newspaper), 74
Colorado, State of, 64, 70
Colored Orphans Home, 173
Colored Women's Federated
 Clubs in St. Louis, 113
Columbia University, 96, 115
Committee on Interracial
 Cooperation, 113
Cùllen, Countee, 179–180

Davis, John, 45
Davis, Sarah Breedlove
 McWilliams; *see* Walker,
 Madam C.J.
Daytona Normal and Industrial
 Institute for Negro Girls, 149
DeMille, Cecil B., 135
Delta, Louisiana, 25, 38
Denver, Colorado, 64, 67–68,
 74, 148
Des Moines, Iowa, 168
Douglass, Frederick, 148
Du Bois, W.E.B., 136, 139,
 150, 152, 172, 179
Dunbar, Paul Laurence, 130

East St. Louis, Illinois, 14,
 138, 140
Elliott, Joan Curl, 64
Emancipation Proclamation, 10
Essence, magazine, 91, 93

Fifteenth Amendment, 32
Fisher, Peg, 90
Fourteenth Amendment, 29
Furniss, Henry Watson, 145

188

Gary, Indiana, 132
Georgia, State of, 173
Great Depression, 119, 182
Greenwood, Mississippi, 39
Grenada, Mississippi, 96
Gross, Stephen, 11

Haines Institute, The, 149, 173
Hall, G. Stanley, 49
Harlem Renaissance, 78, 179, 182
Harlem, New York, 97, 131, 138, 181
Home for Aged and Infirm Colored People, 173
Hot Springs, Arkansas, 133, 166, 167
Howard University Medical School, 113
Hughes, Langston, 179–180, 186
Hunter, Alberta, 179
Hurst, John, 145

Idlewild, Michigan, 132
Indianapolis, Indiana, 96, 135, 155, 179, 182, 188
International League of the Darker Peoples, 152
Irvington-on-the-Hudson, 122–123, 145, 181
Isis Theatre, 135, 179

Jim Crow, 134, 136
Johnson, James Weldon, 136, 139, 145
Joyner, Marjorie, 91–92

Kelly, Alice, 134
Kennedy, A'Lelia McWilliams Walker Robinson Wilson (*nee* Lelia McWilliams), 23–24, 45, 83, 127, 134, 136, 171–172, 181–182
  as support to mother, 178,
  becomes president of Madam C.J. Walker Manufacturing Company, 177

born, 39
dies, 183
divorces John Robinson, 96
divorces Wiley Wilson, 171
enters Knoxville College, 48
graduates college, 78
joins company, 78
marries Dr. James Arthur Kennedy, 171
marries Wiley Wilson, 171
moves to New York, 97
Kennedy, Dr. James Arthur, 171
Kentucky, State of, 104
Kittrell College, 105
Knights of Pythias, 134
Knights of the White Camellia, The, 34
Knoxville College, 78
Knoxville, Tennessee, 48
Ku Klux Klan, 34, 48, 134

Laney, Lucy, 149
Lelia College, 83–84, 97, 112, 178
Lincoln Preparatory School, 115
Long Branch, New Jersey, 186
Los Angeles, California, 132
Louisiana, State of, 23, 25, 34, 62, 70, 75
Lovejoy, Illinois, 108

Madam C.J. Walker Hair Culturists Union of America, 9, 14, 97, 155
Madam Walker Urban Life Center, 188
Majestic Walker Theater, 136, 183
Malone, Aaron, 114
Malone, Annie Turnbo Pope (*nee* Annie Minerva Turnbo), 62, 69, 105, 114, 119
  born, 103
  develops Poro Company, 109

develops hair care products, 105
dies, 103, 115
founds Poro Company, 103
marries Aaron Malone, 113
marries Mr. Pope, 113
philanthropic work, 112
starts Poro College, 112
McWilliams, Lelia; *see* Kennedy, A'Lelia McWilliams Walker Robinson Wilson
McWilliams, Moses (Jeff), 39
McWilliams, Sarah Breedlove; *see* Walker, Madam C.J.
Metropolis, Illinois, 104–105
Mississippi River, 25
Mississippi, State of, 34, 75, 94
Missouri, State of, 64, 94
Moore, Fred, 139, 145
Morgan College, 145
Mother Zion African Methodist Episcopal Zion Church, 172
Muskogee, Oklahoma, 154

Nail, John E., 139
National Association for the Advancement of Colored People (NAACP), 136, 139, 145, 168–169, 181
   Anti-Lynching Conference, 149, 171
National Association of Colored Women, 114, 148
National Beauty Culturists and Benevolent Association; *see* Madam C.J. Walker Hair Culturists Union of America
National Equal Rights League, 150
National Negro Business League, 113, 145, 153–154
National Register of Historic Places, 188
National Youth Administration Program, 119

Negro Associated Press, 108
Nelson, Jill, 90, 94
New Jersey Palisades, 127
New Jersey, State of, 118
New York Age (publication), 14, 75, 139, 145
New York Times (newspaper), 122–123
New York, State of, 75, 118, 122
Nineteenth Amendment, 9, 11
Norfolk Mission College, 115
Norfolk, Virginia, 115
Notable Black American Women (publication), 10, 64

Oklahoma, State of, 75
Ouachita National Forest, 134

Palmer Memorial Institute, 145, 149
Pan-African Congress, 152
Pennsylvania Negro Business Directory (publication), 81
Peoria, Illinois, 105
Philadelphia, Pennsylvania, 9, 14, 115
Phillips, Ellen Douglass, 115
Phillips, Joshua, 115
Pickens, Dean William, 145
Pittsburgh, Pennsylvania, 83–84, 173
Pope, Annie Turnbo; *see* Malone, Annie Turnbo
Poro College, 108
Poro Company, 62–64, 69, 108, 114
Powell, Louvenia Breedlove, 28, 39, 44
Powell, Reverend Adam Clayton, Sr., 139, 152, 186
Powell, Willie, 39, 44

Randolph, A. Phillip, 145
Ransom, Freeman Briley, 90, 94, 130, 133, 135, 152, 169, 173, 182

background, 96
company attorney and manager, 177
Reconstruction, 10, 29, 35, 101, 144
Reynolds, Violet D., 93–94, 97
Robinson, C.K., 170
Robinson, Jessie, 170
Robinson, John, 96
Robinson, Lelia McWilliams Walker; see Kennedy, A'Lelia McWilliams Walker Robinson Wilson
Robinson, Mae (A'Lelia's daughter), 97, 171, 181

Savannah, Georgia, 132
Schieffelin, Colonel William Jay, 152
Scholtz, E.L., 70–71
Schomburg, Arthur, 145
Schuyler, George Samuel, 172
Scott, Emmett J., 145
Sedalia, North Carolina, 149
Social Science History (publication), 11
St. Louis Colored Orphans Home, 113
St. Louis Post Dispatch (newspaper), 53
St. Louis, Missouri, 23, 44, 62–63, 70–72, 108–109, 132, 170, 173
St. Paul African Methodist Episcopal Church, 52
St. Paul's Mite Missionary Society, 53
St. Philip's Episcopal Church, 181

Tandy, Vertner W., 127
The Big Sea: An Autobiography (book), 180
Thirteenth Amendment, 29
Trotter, William Monroe, 150
Tumulty, Joseph, 139

Turnbo, Annie Minerva; *see* Malone, Annie Turnbo
Turnbo, Isabella Cook, 104
Turnbo, Robert, 104
Tuskegee Institute, 113, 173
Twain, Mark, 130

Vicksburg, Mississippi, 25, 38, 44
Villa Lewaro, 131–132, 167–168, 170, 173, 181
Voting Rights Act of 1964, 104

Walker Building, The, 136, 182
Walker College of Beauty Culture, 136
Walker Manufacturing Company, 136
Walker, Charles Joseph, 63
Walker, Madam C.J. (*nee* Sarah Breedlove), 43, 49, 52, 56, 101–104, 108–109, 119, 148, 171, 186–187
  as political activist, 14, 16, 38, 150, 152
  born, 23, 25
  builds Lewaro, 127
  builds factories and laboratories, 86
  death of Moses (Jeff) McWilliams, 39
  declining health, 161–163, 166, 169–170
  denied passport, 152
  develops hair care products, 57, 60, 62, 71–75, 80–81, 84
  dies, 172
  distribution of estate, 173, 174
  divorces John Davis, 45
  divorces Charles Joseph Walker, 78
  early life, 24, 28, 34, 38

entertains at Villa Lewaro, 145
establishes Lelia College, 79
expands to international business, 89, 92
fights discrimination, 135–136, 138–140
fights illiteracy, 143–144
goals, 10–11
incorporates business, 90
invests in real estate, 131–132
learns to read and write, 14
lifestyle, 20
marketing strategy, 16–17, 20, 21
marries Charles Joseph Walker, 71
marries John Davis, 45
marries Moses (Jeff) McWilliams, 39
moves to Denver, Colorado, 67–70
moves to Indianapolis, Indiana, 86
moves to Pittsburgh, Pennsylvania, 79
moves to St. Louis, Missouri, 44
opens beauty parlors nationwide, 88
philanthropic work, 21, 53, 80, 98, 148–149, 168
plans for daughter's future, 24
promotes herself, 153–155, 158
promotes war effort, 169
pursues career, 43
receives honors, 148
spends lavishly, 121–123, 126–127, 130, 132
suffers high blood pressure, 167
works as laundress, 44

works for Annie Turnbo Malone, 63
Walker, Maggie Lena, 145
Ward, Colonel Joseph, 169, 171
Washington, Booker T., 14, 53, 94, 131, 144–145, 153
Washington, D.C., 139
Washington, Margaret Murray, 53, 145
Washington, Sarah Spencer:
  awards, 118
  born, 115
  develops business, 118
  establishes Apex Hair and News Company, 103, 118
  opens hairdressing operation, 115
  philanthropic works, 119
  schooling, 115
Wells-Barnett, Ida B., 126, 145, 150, 167
Western College, 105
White House, 139
White, Walter, 145
Wilson, Lucille, 91
Wilson, President Woodrow, 14, 138–139
Wilson, Lelia McWilliams Walker Robinson; *see* Kennedy, A'Lelia McWilliams Walker Robinson Wilson
Wilson, Wiley, 171
"Women's Duty to Women" (address subject), 10, 155
Woodson, Carter G., 145
Woodson, George, 168
World War I, 150, 171
World's Fair, St. Louis, Missouri, 53, 109

Yellow Fever epidemic, 38
York, Pennsylvania, 115
Young Women's Christian Association (YWCA), 113